THE JOURNEY TO DESTINY-

PROMISE, PROCESS & PERFORMANCE.

ADEMOLA JAMES

Published by:
ADEMOLA JAMES PUBLISHING

ISBN: 978-0-9550679-4-5

London . Lagos

Published in the United Kingdom.

TABLE OF CONTENTS

DEDICATION

This book is dedicated to God Almighty, the creator of heaven and earth, the giver of life, the one that sustained and preserved my life. The one who gave me the enablement and opportunity with great wisdom and insight to write this book during those dark times of my life.

To my lovely, beautiful, and awesome wife Oluwabukunola (TBJ) - for loving, helping, supporting my vision, believing in me and standing by me during my process time. For been my hero, pillar, and a shoulder to cry and lean on during those dark times and wilderness of my life and our marriage. I love you more and more as each day passes by.

To daughter Oluwatimilehin – for your wisdom, suggestions and keeping my company during the writing of this book.

To my daughter Oluwatigbo – for your questioning, each time you see my writing, "daddy what are you doing again, what are you writing"

To my son Oluwatimosin – for your policing and chaperoning your sister ('Tigbo) each time she comes when I was writing and echoing her when she asked those questions.

ACKNOWLEDGEMENT

I thank God Almighty for calling, choosing, and anointed me to be His son and servant, and for inspiring me to impart and impact those around me and becoming a source of encouragement to them all. Also, for the grace to start and complete this work despite everything.

I acknowledge my father, Special Apostle James Adegbuyi Ogundeko who did all his best for me, giving me the education I needed in life; my mother Deaconess Christiana Bamidele Ogundeko (aka Iya Ewe) for her relentless prayers, undying love, her many sacrifices over my life to become what I am today. My father-in-law, Elder Mustapha Durowoju, and my mother-in-law -Mrs Victoria Durowoju (of blessed memory) for their unflinching love and taking me as one of their sons. Evangelist Justina Akinmboni for your motherly love and hospitality when I arrived in the UK.

I acknowledge the unconditional love, support, and prayers of my siblings – Mrs Adeyemi Olaibi, Deaconess Esther Akinmboni, Deaconess Adejoke Oni , Mrs Tolulope Adebowale, Deaconess Mojisola Egbokheo, Mrs Omolola Ojo, and Mr Adedamola James ; thank you all for being there for me.

To my one and only Uncle – Dr Victor Akinsola and his lovely wife – Mrs Funmi Akinsola, a big thank you for your support, encouragement, and guidance over the years. You are both amazing and awesome. I love you both.

To the people who have nurtured, disciplined, taught, inspired, motivated, counselled , encouraged and continuing to do so – my spiritual father who ordained me into ministry, Rev. Matthew Akinjide Daniel and his wife Pastor Mrs Irene Daniel, thank you both for the covering, discipline, teaching, correction and instructions over the years ; my awesome, loving and all round mentor – Dr Charles Omole for your support and wisdom over the years God connected me with you. To all my mentors in different areas of my life – Dr Dayo Olomu, Dr Muyiwa Olumoroti for helping to discover and maximise my potential and for stretching me beyond what I thought was my capacity.

To those who served as my spiritual guide over the years – Pastor JD Modede an uncle and my pastor for several years , your message on Maximizing Potentials inspired my writing of this book, Bishop Bob & Rev (Mrs) Teju Alonge, Pastor Dumebi Jeffreys, Pastor Nick Nunayon, Apostle Oluwole Adekunle, Pastor Tim Femi Oladipo , Evangelist Gboyega Shitta.

To my elders , colleagues and friends in ministry who have in one way or the other made my journey worthwhile – Pastor Emmanuel Iornongu, Apostle Chinwe Onwuchekwa , Pastor Emmanuel Jones, Pastor Joshua Kehinde, Pastor Maxson Akinlade, Pastor Isaac Owusu, Pastor Sam Awonlaogun, Pastor Yomi Odukoya, Pastor (Dr) Henry Akintunde, Pastor Adewale Adeshina, Pastor Kene Nwangwu, Pastor

Emmanuel Folarin, Pastor Afolabi Olanrewaju , Pastor David Oluwole David, Pastor Tunde Arawande, Pastor Bola Arawande (Soar Transcriptions, editor of this book) , Pastor Mayowa Oshin, Pastor Wunmi Shitta, Bishop Wale Ayegbusi, Pastor Yomi Anjorin, Pastor Tayo Taiwo , Minister Olamiju Unuigbo, Psalmist Michael Ekundayo.

To all those God brought my way and have one way or the other being a blessing to me – Temitope & Bunmi Odejobi, Ayodeji & Busola Ayannuga, Adepeju Odusola , Kolapo & Laide Jegede , Minister Ada Nwangwu, Yomi & Bukky Ajomale, Folarin & Biola Ogunbanjo, Benjamin & Dolly Yarere , Goke & Ope Alli , Muyiwa & Funke O'Modede , Ifeoluwa & Damilola Ibileye, Mr Fisayo & Mrs Tope Ademidun and my amiable graphics designer – CJ Benjamin for all your creativity for the book cover.

Thank you all and God bless you richly and abundantly in Jesus name. Amen!

FOREWORD

I have known the Author for many years and in a capacity, that offers me a front row seat into how God has kept him and his family through a series of processes that has led to a God ordained destiny. The reason I stated that was to attest to the authenticity of this book as the writer has poured years of experience into this work.

Promise, Process and Performance details intricately how to navigate from where you are to where God has shown you and especially how to endure when everything screams that you quit or find a less desirable alternative. It gives a map of the different stages and supplies the reader with what to do at each stage of the journey.

I strongly recommend this book to anyone who feels like they have been abandoned and who may be struggling with answers in a very tricky section of their lives. Blessings

Rev Matthew Akinjide Daniel
Global Coordinator
Flaming Sword Ministries UK

PREFACE

Life is a journey, life is a process and life is not roller a coaster. **Adversity in life does not have to become our destination. It can be a pathway to something greater and outstanding.**

Everyone on their way to their promised land will have to go through a process whether they like it or not. God is a God of process and even Jesus went through process - times of suffering when He had to offer prayers and supplications, with loud crying and tears, to the One who is able to save Him from death. (Hebrews 5: 7 NASB)

Every believer in the fulfilment of their destiny or purpose will need to understand that they will go through the wilderness test or a process stage. This is inevitable! Jesus our Lord and Saviour in His human form is our typical example. What we do in our process and how we understand our wilderness test and respond to it may differ from each other. The wilderness is a hard place and it varies among each of us, but it is essential for our lives although it might be painful.

Life is like riding a bicycle, to keep your balance you must keep moving

–

Albert Einstein

While a desert season feels terribly wrong, loneliness and despair may seem to reign, God is with you and He desires to use the wilderness for your eternal good.

To reap its benefits however, you must understand its nature, the purpose and the 'who' is behind it. You will need to also understand how to navigate your process and wilderness state - the spiritual strategy- to go through the process God is taking you through.

You will also need to have a spiritual understanding of the process to see the performance and get the reward of passing your wilderness test because without you passing your wilderness test, there can never be a promotion or performance of God's promises in your life.

You might also need to know why God must take you through a process before the performance of His promises concerning your life. These are the reasons for this book. It will look to the Bible as a "Spiritual Survival Guide" -the supreme source of wisdom both for enduring the wilderness process as well as navigating safely through it to God's promised destination.

God knows how to guide and take care of you as you traverse life's journey, even when it leads you into the wilderness.

There is a process for every promise of God in our lives before the performance of that promise. Do you think that the tough things, situation you have passed through or presently going through are always an indication that you are not on the right path?

If you do, you may be wrong because this is often not the case. Do you also ponder on the difficulties in life you are going through as an evidence of God's disapproval or that you have sinned against God? This book is written to guide you through your process

We far too easily assume that because God has called us and has His hand upon us, everything will go without any hitch or contest.

When God has a divine plan for you, choose you or set you apart, some lions will come your way. There is a dimension of opposition and pressure that comes your way when you align yourself with the will, plan, and purpose of God for your life. There are certain things that must be present in your life to prepare and process you for every good work and qualify you to see God's promises over your life.

God will surely take you through some certain things in life called process which leads to performance, and these things vary from one season of your life to another season of your life. God has prepared a table before you, but you will need to understand the path, system, and process that God has planned for you to dine at the table He set for you.

The process God will take you through is not the destination, the process is a preparation, part of your journey in the fulfilment of your destiny, the performance of God's glory in your life.

The journey into destiny is a pathway we must follow to see the performance of God's promises over our lives, it is the way to follow for us to experience the greatness th at God has promised us. This book is an in-depth analysis of the process God will take you through to see the performance of His promises. It begins with promises of God, founded upon conviction of those promise, it is sustained by preparation, it will require patience, faith, courage, obedience, and it brings about performance and its fulfilment.

So therefore, join me as we take this journey together into destiny fulfilment – Promise, Process and Performance.

It promises to be an inspiring and transformative journey as we take a deep read into how to endure every challenging situation as we eagerly await the fulfilment and performance of God's promises.

God bless you
Be transformed and empowered.

ADEMOLA JAMES

CHAPTER 1

THE PROMISE

The word "promise" is a word we use often and times without number. Unfortunately, it is a word that most people do not have an in-depth meaning of, or full understanding of.

In this chapter, I will be laying a foundation of this book by looking deeply at what "promise" really means. One thing we need to understand first is that God is a God of promise and all His promises are yea and amen. "*For all the promises of God in Him are yea and in Him Amen unto the glory of God by us* – **2 Cor 1:20"**
The Scriptures says "…all the promises of God **in Him**…" - not in anyone else, but in Him, are yea (yes) and in Him amen (it is done). This is

simply saying to us that all of God's promises to us is of certainty. They will surely come to pass. There shall be a performance of all God's promises to us and the fulfilment will only happen in Him.

All His Promises Are Yea and Amen

The Word of God also says, *"God is not a God that should lie nor son of man that would repent."* In other words, when God promises anything, He will surely fulfil it. God does not lie, we can trust Him with whatever He promises us either through His Word or prophecy given to us by His prophets, if it is in accordance to His will for our lives.

You see God is not human that He will promise you and not fulfil that which He had promised us. We, as human, can promise something today and by tomorrow retract the promise or fail to fulfil that promise we made at times because of circumstances beyond us. Some retract their promises because of lack of integrity. However, God is not like us- human, He is not fickle in His decisions. He will always fulfil His promises to us, and we can confidently rely on Him and His Words anytime, any day.

When the Bible says all His promises are yea and amen, it is simply saying they are all done deal. They are all yes. It will happen, and it is settled. Amen simply means “so shall it be”. So, God promises, all His promises are all “so shall it be”.

So, let us go deeper into what the word ‘promise’ is all about. The Oxford Dictionary defines ‘promise’ as:

- A declaration or assurance that one will do something or that a thing will happen.
- Assure someone that one will do something or that something will happen.
- To give good grounds for expecting a occurrence.

The Origin - late Middle English: from Latin promissum 'something promised', neuter past participle of promittere 'put forth, promise', from pro- 'forward' + mittere 'send'

From the definition, we can then say that the promises of God concerning us or when God promises us, it is a declaration or assurance that God will do something for us or a particular thing will happen to us.

The Word of God in the Bible are full of promises, assurances, and declaration of what He can do and will do for us. Hence why it is very imperative for us to read, study and meditate on the Word of God because it is full of assurances from God concerning every area of our lives.

There are various promises of God in the Bible that God has promised and covenanted to bring to pass. He will bring all to performance in our lives.

Promises of God

When you study the word of God, with the help of the Holy Spirit, you will understand and agree with me that from the beginning (Genesis) to the end (Revelation), it is full of God's unfailing and unshaken promises concerning His children (believers in Christ) and the creation.

These promises are diverse and different and cut across all spheres of our lives – health, financial, marriage, children, family, nations, church, and the body of Christ. Each of these promises speaks to each of us according to our situation or circumstances and they are also general promises. They are promises we can personalise for ourselves as well.

Let God's promises shine on your problem and circumstances.

God's Word is filled with His promises for every area of our lives. The Bible is the ultimate source of truth and God is faithful to fulfil all His promises. As you read through the Scripture about the promises of God, claim them over your life. Freedom from every form of addiction, deliverance from sin and evil, financial provision, hope for the lost, and hurting family and friends, overcoming depression, restoration of marriage, good health, healing, freedom from fear and anxiety, strength and many more, are the blessings and gifts God promises to provide for those who believe in Him.

There are many promises of God in the Scripture that we can claim over our lives. In each promise, God pledges that something will be done or given or come to pass. These are not flippant, casual promises such as we often make.

These promises are rock-solid, unequivocal commitment made by God Himself. God is faithful; therefore, the recipients of the divine promises can have full assurance that what He has pledged will indeed be materialised. **(Numbers 23: 19)**

Do you know that there are over 3000 promises of God in the Bible?

Humility is to believe God's Word over your circumstances and carnal logic. It is often difficult to pluck up courage to believe, but you can be rest assured if you are in Christ. God is seeking to make His promises a reality in your life for His glory. How can those in Christ experience His promises? Look at the second part of - **2 Corinthians 1: 20 (NIV)** *" So through Him the Amen is spoken by us to the glory of God"*

Amen means to establish. This means you have a part to play in the establishment of God's promises in your life. You could say it this way – "God's promises are established in your life as you speak them. But not just speak them, believe they are yours because you are in Christ. The grace to receive promises manifest as your heart is persuaded of the truth that ALL of God's promises are YES and Amen in Christ.

Here are just few of the promises that God has made:

Promises of God in the Old Testament

God promised to bless Abraham and through his descendants- the whole world would be blessed (Genesis 12:2–3). This promise called the Abrahamic covenant pointed to the coming Messiah for whom Abraham looked (John 8:56).

God promised Israel to be their God and make them His people (Leviticus 26:12–13). Old Testament history teems with examples of God fulfilling this promise.

God promised that if we search for Him, we will find Him (Deuteronomy 4:29). He is not playing hard-to-get. "Our God is near us whenever we pray to Him" (Deuteronomy 4:7).

God promised protection for His children (Psalm 121). He was the vigilant watchman over all Israel.

God promised that His love will never fail (1 Chronicles 16:34). He is faithful in every way.

God promised Israel that their sin could be forgiven, their prosperity restored, and their nation healed (2 Chronicles 7:14). Repentance opened the road to fellowship and blessing.

God, under the terms of the Mosaic Covenant, promised prosperity to Israel for obedience, and destruction for disobedience (Deuteronomy 30:15–18). Unfortunately, Israel eventually chose to disobey God and the nation was destroyed by Assyria and Babylon.

God promised blessing for all who will delight themselves in His Word (Psalm 1:1–3). Simple faith has its rewards.

Promises of God in the New Testament

God promised salvation to all who believe in His Son (Romans 1:16–17). There is no greater blessing than the gift of God's salvation.

God promised that all things will work out for good for His children (Romans 8:28). This is the broader picture that keeps us from being dismayed by present circumstances.

God promised comfort in our trials (2 Corinthians 1:3–4). He has a plan, and one day we will be able to share the comfort we receive with others who will hence be comforted by our stories.

God promised new life in Christ (2 Corinthians 5:17). Salvation is the beginning of a brand-new existence.

God promised to finish the work He started in us (Philippians 1:6). God does nothing in half measures. He started the work in us, and He will be sure to complete it.

God promised peace when we pray (Philippians 4:6–7). His peace is protection. It will "guard your hearts and your minds in Christ."

God promised to supply our needs (Matthew 6:33; Philippians 4:19). We are more valuable than the birds, and our heavenly Father feeds them (Matthew 6:26).

Jesus' promises in the Gospels

Jesus promised rest (Matthew 11:28–30). Burdens are lifted at Calvary.

Jesus promised abundant life to those who follow Him (John 10:10). Following Jesus brings us more spiritual fulfilment than we could have anticipated. We leave boring behind!

Jesus promised eternal life to those who trust Him (John 4:14). The Good Shepherd also promised to hold us securely: "***No one will snatch them out of my hand***" (John 10:28).

Jesus promised His disciples power from on high (Acts 1:8). In this power, they "***turned the world upside down***" (Acts 17:6, ESV).

Jesus promised that He will return for us (John 14:2–3). From then on, we will be with Him always.
There are many more promises of God that could be listed. All of them find their ultimate fulfilment in Jesus Christ, "the radiance of God's glory" (Hebrews 1:3). "No matter how many promises God has made, they are 'Yes' in Christ" (2 Corinthians 1:20).

The Word of God are His promises to you. Discovering them is discovering a great treasure. As you keep digging into it, you will find more and more amazing and beautiful treasures.

God is a God of promise. Faith involves trusting the promises of God. God makes a promise, faith believes it; hope anticipates it; patience quietly waits for it.

MODES OF HIS PROMISES

Aside that the promises of God are generic in nature, the promises in the Bible are for everyone who believes. Every believer can claim them.

God also gives us specific promises based on our calling and purpose in life. These specific promises can be given to us by God through different modes to deliver it to us and make us aware of them. Let us consider some of the ways God makes His promises known to us:

1. **His Word** – As I have said earlier, the Word of God contains the promises of God and when we read, study and meditate upon it diligently, we get a glimpse of the future He has for us- His plan and purpose for our individual life.

2. **Revelation:** God sometimes gives us a promise through revelation. Where we cut a vivid picture of His future for us in a glance. Revelation is a divine or supernatural disclosure to humans of something relating to human existence. It means unveiling or disclosure of something previously hidden. Your future is hidden in God but through revelation God can unveil or disclose it

to you and you can hold on to this as His promise.

3. **Dream:** God can give you a promise through a dream. For example, Joseph received the promise of God through a dream. He dreamt that he would become an important person in Egypt and his brothers will bow down to him one day. Joseph held on to that dream as God promise to him.

4. **Word of Knowledge:** God works in diverse ways. For instance, you may be trusting God for the fruit of the womb or marital settlement and He can give you His promise by a word of knowledge through a servant of His.

5. **Prophecy:** You can be prophesied upon, concerning an issue in your life. Maybe your immigration status , fruit of the womb or whatever it could be, as long as the prophecy is in accordance to

> God's will for your life , you can hold on to this prophecy as His promise to you and believe that it will come to pass and be fulfilled in your life.

God works in promises; he deals in making new things out of the old. All throughout biblical history, we see the hand of the Almighty heavy with promises to his beloved. Generations later, we are not exempted from those promises made so many years ago. *As you read the Ephesians and Corinthians passages, note what promises of God you see. Examine them closely.*

God's promises have a very specific nature to them. Yes, they are for our benefit and His glory, and yet in His divine workings, they are also designed as faith builders that helps in bringing us closer to Him, nurturing our relationship more, wooing us- His bride further into His arms.

Timeframes, expectations, unknown destinations, leaps of faith- all these can be utilised in His ultimate plan for us. Sometimes we know where we are called, other times we are just instructed to start_walking. Sometimes we get a peek at the supernatural schedule, other times we travel without an itinerary. Sometimes we need to only obey, and little faith is required; other times we cannot do anything but sit, rest, and wait faithfully- doing nothing but believing God to move. Often, it is a mixture of all these and more. It is no wonder Abraham made it into the hall of faith in Hebrews 12. He faced all these trials and more!

Now that we have established the promises of God, you need to understand that these promises do not just happen overnight or in a twinkling of an eye. The promises of God take time to come to pass or fulfilled. The time in between the declaration of promises and the fulfilment is what is called PROCESS OR PREPARATION.

You need to understand if you want to see the promises of God and its manifestation, you will be ready to go through a PROCESS and allow

God to PREPARE you for the performance of His promises to you.

CHAPTER 2

THE PROCESS

God has a wonderful way of disguising opportunities as problems. There is a need to understand that life is a process and before you experience the performance of the promises of God concerning your life, process is necessary and essential. There is no one God promised anything without going through a certain process before experiencing the manifestation of what He promised them.

For instance, when God promised Abraham that he would be a father of many nations, although

God can make it happen within a space of time, but it did not just happen. He had to take Abraham through a process or a preparation time before He fulfilled that which He had promised Abraham.

You cannot experience the performance of the promise without the process.

Process can also mean preparation, this a period where God prepare you for that which He had promised you. I have not seen anyone either in the Bible or on this earth that has not gone through a process before they become what they are today. Their stories before their glory is their process or preparation time.

It is very unfortunate that in these days we live in, we want to avoid the process and obtain the promise at the snap of fingers. We are now living in a microwave world, where we want to experience instant or overnight success without going through the preparation period.

Process is very essential if we want the performance to be sustainable and the promise to be weighty. Hence, we must avoid premature success or fulfilment of the promise that has not gone through a process or preparation period.

My own personal life and story is a typical example of a process that I believe it is essential for us to go through in our walk with God to lay hold of His promise concerning us as believers.

In subsequent chapter, I will share my story, the process God took me through, lessons I learnt and how He performed that which He promised me. This is the whole purpose of this book, also by the inspiration of the Spirit of God, He gave me words for each letter in the word **"PROCESS".** The acronym - PROCESS, is what forms the next seven chapters of this book.

This will also give an understanding and insight to why you will need to take your process or preparation period seriously because if you do not understand the purpose of a thing, you will abuse that thing. If you do not have a clue about why God is taking you through a process or preparation period, there is tendency that you will not take it seriously, you will live a victimised life and will also be complacent in the process. Understanding is the key to everything in this life.

There is always a beginning to everything in life and every beginning has an end. Each of us in this life, begins somewhere at one point in time. There is no secret to success. It is the result of preparation, hard work and learning from failure hence why you need to see your process stage as a preparation for the performance of the promise.

If you are waiting on God's promise to be performed and fulfilled in your life, do not look for shortcuts. Decide and be determined to go through the process God will take you through.

As someone said that ***shortcut is always the longest route to success***.

Being a Christian does not exempt us from trouble or discomfort. We have do not have immunity from challenges in life.

Remember what Jesus said in John 16: 33 - *These things I have spoken unto you, that in me ye might have peace. In the world ye shall have tribulation: but be of good cheer; I have overcome the world.*

Jesus is simply saying to us that we will surely have discomfort, tribulations, challenging times, and sufferings as long as we are in this world, whether we like it or not. Despite all the difficulties, He gave us an assurance and a comforting word that we should be of good cheer. This means 'have courage', 'be unshakeable', 'be assured and deeply at peace' because He has overcome the world and all challenges and issues of life on our behalf.

Therefore, in our process or preparation period there will be difficulty and discomfort, but we must decide and be determined to go through it so that we can come out like gold. The process period is our testing and trying times as Job 23: 10 says - *But he knoweth the way that I take: when he hath tried me, I shall come forth as gold.*

Gold is a beautiful product that we all love to have in our possession. But as beautiful as it is, most do not know the process it has gone through. We only see the finished product and we are not concerned about the process the gold has passed through, if it is beautiful, and we can afford it, we just buy it. Hence original gold is costly.

GOLD SMELTING PROCESS

Gold Smelting

Gold is purified by means of a smelting process, which utilises pressure, high heat, and chemicals to accomplish the task. Like any metal that appears naturally in the earth, there are impurities that must be removed. Removing minerals and other impurities allows gold to be used in its purest form, which is necessary in many applications, particularly in jewellery and electronics. Gold is utilised frequently for electronic applications because it does not tarnish or rust over time.

Ore Processing

The first step in the gold smelting process occurs when ore containing gold is mined from the earth. At this point, the crude binding matter and the gold metal need to be separated. This is accomplished by pulverizing or crushing the gold ore, and then placing it in a furnace. The furnace must reach temperatures in excess of 1064 degrees Celsius, in order to elevate the gold above its melting point.

Removing Impurities

While many impurities are burned off in the furnace, other metals remain. Gold ore extracted from mines in the earth contains a significant amount of impurities, including traces of other metals. To separate the gold from other metals, chemicals such as cyanide solution or mercury are introduced to the gold. This process causes the gold to coagulate, and form nuggets and clumps of gold.

Use of Purified Gold

After the gold smelting process is complete, the gold is melted once more, and poured into mould to form ingots. Later, the gold ingots may be used for various purposes fulfilled best by this precious metal. Some of these golds are used for jewellery and electronics and may later be recycled for other uses. If gold from jewellery or electronics is to be recycled, the scrap gold must go through another smelting process to be considered pure once more.

Many of us do not want to go through purification, smelting process, like how the gold goes through refining process. We want to have a glory without a story.

No glory without a story. No story, No glory!

Our story is the process and preparation we will go through while our glory are the manifestations as we come out as gold- becoming attractive to others as gold is attractive to everybody.

Romans 8: *18 – 19 says "For I reckon that the sufferings of this present time are not worthy to be compared with the glory which shall be revealed in us. For the earnest expectation of the creature waiteth for the manifestation of the sons of God."*

This is simply talking about a future glory that God wants to reveal in our lives, but it will not just happen without us going through the process. This process comes in different shapes and sizes, also sufferings and discomfort forms part of this process for our glory to be revealed.

We need to understand that we must allow God to purify, mould and remove all impurities in our lives during our process period before He will then reveal the glory in us and bring us to the manifestations intended for us.

Preparation comes before promotion, if not humiliation will follow.

God's plan is always the best. Sometimes the process is very painful and hard, but do not forget that when God is silent, He is doing something for you and in you. The process involved before one experience the performance of the promise can be full of discouragement and excruciating pain. Hence patience, faith and perseverance are essential. **(We will look at these three later).**

During the process, your character is formed to sustain the performance and to make the manifestation last longer. God is so much interested in our transformation and character development as much as He is interested in our comfort. Therefore, the process is of necessity so that our character can be formed.

You do not change or grow when everything is easy, and you do not learn anything when everything is easy too.

We often think of waiting as negative, no one like it when nothing is happening. No one likes the process period. Although we are so much interested in the destination, but God is interested in both the process and our destination. He is working in us along the way.

I truly believe that every single person must go through something that absolutely 'destroys' them so they can figure out who they really are. It is during this process period, one learns and discovers one's identity, capability, potential and what one is made of.

When the blessing or promise seems to be delayed, God is working on you and your character. The blessing is the reward that comes after you have learnt obedience through the things you suffered while waiting for it.

To live, something must die. To give birth, a mother must endure the suffering of the birth process. Before God promotes us, He takes us through pain to purify our hearts, deepen our dependence on Him and impart spiritual wisdom.

Pain comes before Promotion.
Whatever pain you might be going through at this moment is for your own good. It is a way of God processing, moulding, and shaping you to become a better person and come out as gold.
Nothing that happens to you takes God by surprise. He is aware of everything and He is using whatever you are going through to prepare you for what He has already prepared for you.

You would be surprised who is watching your journey, your process period, and being inspired by it. Do not quit!

You must understand that where you are NOW is not as importance as where you are going. The destination God is taking you to is far more important. Hence you need Him to process and work in you for the glory to be revealed in you and through you.

Your best stories will come through your struggles, pains, and battles. The seeds of your success are in your failures and disappointments. Your praises will be birthed from your pains.
Your greatest ministry (service) comes from your deepest pain, and your pain is hidden in your process.

When things are not working as you expect them to be, take is as God's subtle way of teaching you to grow in your walk in and with Christ. The process may be difficult, but it will surely bring the best out of you. It is true that there will always be some crows in your lives pecking at you, trying to bait you into a fight, the only way to argue with a crow is to come down to their level. However, always remember that You are an eagle. Quit wasting your time with crows.

In life there must be preparation, readiness then victory. You may be wondering that if God has better plans for you, how come you do not have it? The truth is that God is not waiting to try to build a better life for you. The better life is already available in Him. He needs to build you up so that you can fit in perfectly to what He has already built for you. He can only do this through your process period. Do not be discouraged in the process, and about the process if God is in the process.

Sometimes, where you are now is where God needs you to be. He is preparing you for your destiny. God does everything with excellence, trust the process. If you are believing God for something and it seems like it is taking far too long, do not give up. HOLD ON.

God wants the best for you. ***He must prepare you before He promotes you***. Keep doing the right thing. Trust God. His grace is sufficient.

God is a God of process. It is the process one is subjected to that determines one's value in life, ministry, and marketplace. Joseph had to go through process and preparation before he became the Prime Minister in a foreign land. He was sold as a slave by his brothers, wrongly accused of sexually assaulting his boss' wife and imprisoned.

The wilderness is your journey to fulfilment and performance of what God had already promised you.

David Oluwole David, in his book – Knock Down but not Knock Out mentioned that:

> *"...there is going to be a momentary period of our lives when we feel forsaken. Such times when you look at yourself and wonder, 'Where is God?' 'Doesn't He answer prayers anymore?' 'But I can pray!'..." you proclaimed. Of course, you can pray, you know how to worship God in truth and in spirit, you know how to spend and be spent for Christ as instructed by Apostle Paul. You love God with all your heart, yet it seems as if He has forsaken you. Be assured that you are not the first and you will not be the last that has been forsaken. It is just for a moment. It is a 'knock down', and it is just for a short while. You must realise that "God*

is more interested in moulding your character than making you happy."

Jesus cried out in Mark 15:34-
"And at the ninth hour, Jesus cried out with a loud voice, saying, "Eloi, Eloi, lama sabachthani?" which is translated, "My God, My God, why have You forsaken Me?

If God could forsake His only begotten Son momentarily, He will forsake you at some point, not as a punishment but as part of a training, as a soldier in His army. A soldier who will learn to fight with all armours, focused on his assignment and ready to bear the pains of his special calling or assignment.

Remember, a path without obstacles leads nowhere.

Do not run from the process that leads to the performance of your glory, promotion, and manifestation. There is no way for you to shorten the wilderness God designed for you, but you sure can lengthen it through your attitude towards the wilderness and your perception of the process. One thing you need to understand is that, going through the process or wilderness does not mean you are off course or not in the centre of God's will.

God is preparing you for something great. God knows the plans He has for us. But the process to get to those plans takes time. We can get impatient with the process while we wait for the promises of God. God wants His plans and promises to be a blessing and if we receive it prematurely, we will not have the character to keep it.

The waiting period between when God answers your prayers and when you receive is where Christian character development occurs.

God is preparing you for more. Make room for your future. God loves you too much not to give you the promotion without the pruning. He is a just and loving God. You cannot be promoted by

God and not be pruned. All that were used by God in the Bible, for instance- Abraham, Joseph, David, and Paul formerly known as Saul, were all pruned before they were promoted. If you faint in the process, you will never fulfil your destiny and experience the performance of the promise.

The process can be days, weeks, months, even years of adversity and you cannot afford to be faint. You need to gather inner strength and it can only be from God for by strength shall no man prevail. The joy of the Lord must be your strength during your process period.

Trust the Process

One thing is for sure, the beginning of the process usually looks nothing like the finished product of the process. Therefore, trust the process. It will all make total sense one day. Process is the alignment between confusion and clarity. Only those who pay attention excel at the end of the process. Allow God to prepare you so that you can enter the performance of His promise. You cannot experience the performance of the promise without the process. I say again and again, trust the process.

Let me make something clear. Not all process or wilderness experiences are the same. Some are caused by sin or disobedience and some are Holy Spirit training exercises. We therefore must know what kind of wilderness we are in so we can know how to respond to it. There will be a need to assess our situation to determine what type of process we are in.

What happens to us is not the problem, but the problem is how we respond to what happens to us.

When God wants to promote us to a new level in life, He does not just whisk us into position. He prepares, trains, and refines us before He can lift us into a new dimension of our destiny. If we resist the process, we resist the promotion. It is that simple. The wilderness is the process. It is a dry, difficult time when God stripes us of self-support and compels us to look to Him in a new way. God does not want superficial people. He does not want children who know to act spiritual in Church or when life is easy, but when serious pressure or injustice comes, react just as the world would. God wants a people like His Son – Jesus, fully developed. Spiritual people who have gone through raw wasteland and emerged shining like gold and stars – *"when He has tested me, I shall come forth as gold" - Job 23:10*

God's hammer and chisel forge into such people real's character, faith, and maturity. They have had a genuine, ground level experience with God. Now they look like Jesus: meek, loving, powerful and real. You cannot get such results quickly. You cannot get them cheaply. They come only through God's painful cauldron, pruning, processing, and result in the sweet Spirit of Christ's character.

Before Joseph fulfilled his dream of greatness, he was moulded in the dry outback of rejection, pit, and prison. Through it all, he remained loyal to God and became the most powerful man in the world, next to Pharaoh. But he had to be prepared for such glory to be revealed in him.

Before promotion, there must be process; before resurrection, there must be death.

Let the process mould you into Christ's image. You will have great reward and fulfil your destiny. As Smith Wigglesworth said, "***only melted gold is minted.***"

The Power of Process

1. There is a process for every promise.
2. Process is the period God empty you of yourself. So that God can refill you.
3. Process is more about you as a person, God changing your focus to Him.
4. Process is a way your trust in God is built and it allows you to trust God.
5. Process is a way you trust God even he does not do anything for you.
6. Transformation and conforming to the image of the person of Jesus Christ comes through process.

7. The whole essence of the process is to make God your reliance and dependence.
8. Process is what built in you the necessary character, virtue, and spiritual stamina to sustain the blessings and the performance of the promises of God concerning you.
9. Process is preparation time.
10. Process produces character.
11. Process produces stature to function.
12. Process produces capacity to carry the future you have seen, and God uses process to achieve this.
13. The process is the preparation for your victory
14. Without the process, the performance (fulfilment) will not carry the weight of the promise.
15. Focus on the PROCESS not just the DESTINATION. The process is KEY to the destination.

CHAPTER 3

PURPOSE AND PREPARATION.

God is a God of purpose and He never allows any pain or process without a purpose for it. To come out of your process and well prepared for the performance of the promise excellently, you will need to first discover what the purpose of the process God is taking you through is.

What is the purpose of my wilderness experience? What is in the mind of God for allowing me to go through the waiting and hurting period?

Failure to discover the purpose of your process will not yield any result and you will not pass the wilderness test nor experience the performance of the promise. You will keep on repeating the class, going around in circles. God never allows a pain without a purpose. You need to understand that the wilderness you are currently going through has a purpose. Everything in God and with Him has a purpose. Nothing happens by accident as far as God is concerned.

God never allows any pain without a purpose

The process stage you are currently in has its own purpose. God will never allow you to go through any process or wilderness without a purpose for it. It is very imperative that you discover the purpose of God in the state you are in right now.

Everything in life has a purpose and God is a God of purpose, God is an intentional God. Intentionality is one of the natures of God. He has an intention for you and a "why" for you to be going through what you may be going through now.

Whatever the situation is, God has a purpose for it. No matter how bad, discomforting or discouraging the situation is, God has a purpose for allowing it in your life. Hence it is very important for you to ask God in the place of prayer. Why did He allow this in your life and what is He is teaching you? What does He want you to learn, what life lessons do you have to learn?

When you study or read the Bible carefully, you would agree with me that everything God created has its own purpose. Nothing is by accident. The Sun, moon, light, darkness, animal, ocean, water, forest, trees etc. Name that thing under the heaven that does not have purpose.

In Ecclesiastes 3 vs 1, it says *"To everything there is a season and a time to every purpose under the heaven.*

This clearly shows us that the process you are in right now or the process God is taking you through now has its own purpose. He is not taking you through it because He hates you or punishing you, especially if you are in Christ and Christ is in you. He is taking you through it for a particular purpose and it is very essential that you know the purpose of your process, "the why".

When you know the "why" of the process, it will assist you in knowing what to do, how to navigate it and which direction you need to take during the process period.

Take Abraham for example, he was barren, had no child for several years even though God had promise him that he would be father of many nations. Then God had to take Him through a process whereby He told him to leave his father's house to a land He would show him.

God had something in mind and knew why He had to instruct Moses to leave his father's house to somewhere he was unfamiliar with. God had a purpose, an intention in His mind. You would agree with me that the purpose of that in the case of Abraham was to prepare the birth of our Lord Jesus Christ. There is no one that God promised that would not go through a process before the performance of the promise.

There is always a purpose for your pain and discomfort.

As you go through your wilderness stage, have it at the back of your mind that there is a purpose for this process, and you must discover that purpose. This is very key and important. If you do not, you will not be able to maximise the opportunities (I will expand on this in another chapter) embedded in the process.

Purpose has been defined as the original intent for the creation of a thing that is in the mind of the creator of that thing (Late Dr Myles Munroe)

Nothing in life is without a purpose. God does not think without a purpose. So, your question to God in your wilderness stage is "What is the original intent in the mind of God for this situation you are in now?" If you want to know the purpose of a thing, never ask the thing. Who do you ask? You ask the creator of the thing. Why? Because the purpose of a thing can only be found in the mind of the creator of that thing.

Time is too short. The best way to waste time is by not knowing the purpose of anything. If you do not know the purpose of the process you are in, you would waste a lot time crying, complaining, and moaning. You would waste so much time competing, comparing, and envying others.

Purpose is the reason for which something is done or created or for which something exists. There is a purpose for why you are existing, why you are where you are now; still alive till this present moment and there is also a purpose why the process you are in now exists.

Let us consider few principles of Purpose.

1) God is a God of purpose.
2) God created everything with, and for a purpose in mind
3) Not every purpose is known to us because we have lost our understanding of God's original intention for us.
4) Where purpose is not known, abuse is unavoidable.
5) To discover purpose of something never ask the creation, ask the creator.
6) We find our purpose only in the mind of our maker.
7) God's purpose is the key to our fulfilment.

For the intention behind this book, I would highlight some of the purpose I believe are the reasons why we go through what we go through in life. This is what we call wilderness experience. The reason God allows us to go through the process, and why He must take us through process. Remember I said earlier, that everything has its own purpose and I strongly believe that whatever state you are in and see as discomforting or suffering, there is a purpose for it and why God allows it to happen.

Come to think of it, God is all-powerful and omnipotent God, He has the power not to allow you go through it, but He decides that you will have to go through it. So, for that to happen, believe me, and without any iota of doubt, I strongly believe that there is a reason or many reasons for it.

So, let us look at few reasons why God would allow or make us to go through the process or wilderness period.

1. ***His Glory***. He is God of glory. For Him to reveal His glory in us and through us and for the glory to manifest, sometimes He will test and try us, and allow us to go through some certain things in life.

2. ***Character Development***. You see, at times, when the blessing is delayed, God is working on us and our character. Our character is more important to God than the blessing itself. We need to remove the impurities in us, so He will need to use our time of process to purify and mould us. ***All trials can be used by God to refine us and draw us closer to Him. Character is not built in pleasure. Character is built in pains. The waiting period between when God answers our prayers and when we tangibly receive the answer is where Christian development occurs.***

3. ***Transformation:*** Our total transformation is key and important to God. Transforming us to the image of Christ is the key objective for God. You may bc going through fire, but God wants to bring you out on the other side, better than you were before, a transformed person. This is my testimony when He took me through my wilderness stage.

4. ***Dependence on Him:*** God is an intentional God. He wants to deepen our dependence on

Him. You see every problem provides us with the opportunity to know God better and grow in dependence of Him.

5. ***To get our attention:*** I love God so much that He will sometimes cause disruption in our lives to get our attention. I can testify to this, and this has been my case. You remember Jonah, God had to cause the ship to be capsized to get Jonah's attention when he thought he had run away from God. ***God whispers to us through our blessings, speak to us through our hardship and shouts at us through our* suffering*. God gets our attention through our sufferings, problems and trials.***

6. ***Intimate Relationship***: God desires an intimate relationship with us, and He wants us to know Him deeper than we think we know Him. So, at times He allows us to go through the process for us to seek Him diligently and build a relationship with Him even in our discomforting state. The Holy Spirit wants to lead us into a deeper, intimate experience with God.

Everything from our perspective changes in His presence.

Romans 8 vs 28 -30 are verses of the Bible that gives us a full summary of the reason why we go through the process or the wilderness stage. All things (including that situation you are in now) works together for good. At the end of the day, it is for our good, though it might be challenging, tough or difficult but believe me it is for our own good.

Joseph told his brothers that even though they meant it for evil, but God meant it for good. The "**it**" in the passage is all that happened to him – slavery , the lie against him, the imprisonment, all what hc went through , the process God took him through , the preparation stage , the wilderness , the difficult times , they were all evil but God allowed it for good.

Take Jesus as another example, all what He went through , spitting on Him, stoning, lies against Him, the rejection, the betrayal , death on the cross , burial , resurrection- they were all for good , for His glory and the prophecy to be fulfilled. The good here is the glory of God. Every believer who loves God, and that has gone through any wilderness experience in life is all for good, to the glory of God.

Take it Serious

"There is a call of God upon every one of us and we need to take this call serious. This call places a greater responsibility on our shoulders. I know where I have been and where I am at this moment and I give God the glory for where He is taking me to. It is indeed an honour and privilege that God has chosen me despite my weakness, flaws, imperfections, and unrighteousness. I have gone through a wilderness stage and by His grace and mercy I am grateful for how far He has brought me and how His grace abounds towards me to go through that process stage of my life. He has indeed brought me a long way.

Do not ever be intimidated by the calling of any other person. Never try to replicate another person's encounter. Each of us process is unique" – Francis Bob Alonge (The Making of a Chosen Vessel)

Everyone's purpose is different from each other. Hence, we must not dare to compare our lives or where we are now with another person. We dare not envy or be jealous of anyone. Why? Because we will all go through the process stage, but at different times in our lives.

The process stage humbles us if we can allow it to do the work of internal transformation in us that will be evident on the outside. There is a perfect work God wants to do in our lives through our trials and difficult times.

Everything that happens to us can be used by God to advance His purposes in our lives.

When God bring it all together, it is not going to be what you think. It is going to be bigger. better and more rewarding than you ever expected. In the wilderness stage, the dry times, you must learn to seek God for who He is rather than what He can do for you. It is the period to know Him personally and this might be one of the many purposes of the wilderness stage of your life.

PREPARATION

In the process period, preparation is very crucial for the performance to take place. Therefore, see the process as a preparation for the performance of the promise. ***Your preparation will determine your acceleration hence your arrival time.*** Preparation time is not a wasted time, do not be deceived by this 'get it quick' syndrome. Prepare well to arrive and perform, to sustain the performance of the blessing and the promise. ***Preparation precedes destination.***

"When things are not working as what you expect them to be, take it as God's subtle way of teaching you to grow and prepare you. The process may be difficult, but it will surely bring the best out of you. It is true that there will always

be some crows in our lives pecking at us, trying to bait you into a fight. But the only way to argue with a crow is to come down to their level. You are an eagle, quit wasting your time with crows." – TD Jakes

In life there must be preparation and readiness, then victory. David's victory over Goliath was well prepared in advance, he was ever ready before he eventually faced Goliath. David had gone through a preparation in His process period, he had killed a bear, fought a lion and he was abandoned in the farm to care for his father's cattle all by himself. All these were his preparation and readiness for his victory over Goliath.

"You may be wondering that if God got better for me, how come I don't have it. Reason is because better a performance of a promise that you have prepared for. You see the better is prepared but the receiver is not prepared. God is not waiting to try to build a better life for you. the better life is already built. He is trying to build

you up so that can fit what He has already built" – TD Jakes

Walking in purpose sometimes means waiting as much as it means moving forward. A lot of depth is built in period of waiting and preparation. Do not be discouraged about the process, God is in the process. Where you are now is where God needs you to be. He is preparing you for your destiny. God does everything with excellence, trust the process. If you are believing God for anything or something and it seems like it is taking too long do not give up. HOLD ON.

Preparation comes before Elevation

God wants the best for you however He must prepare you before He promotes you. Keep doing the right thing. Trust God. His grace is enough. God is a God of process. It is the process you are subjected to that determines your value in life and how valuable you will become. The wilderness is your journey to promise fulfilled, a performance of what He had already promised you. ***Do not run from the process that leads to the***

performance of the promise, your promotion and manifestation.

"There is no way for you to shorten the wilderness God designed for you but you sure can lengthen it through your attitude towards the wilderness and your perception of the process" – John Bevere

You must understand that going through the wilderness or the process does not mean you are off course or not at the centre of God's will. It is God's preparing you for what He had promised you.

Often when you end up in a wilderness, it is easy to think you went wrong somewhere – that somehow you missed God's plan. On the contrary, it is God who leads us into the wilderness and ultimately through it. There is purpose in you been there. God wants to use the wilderness season to develop and prepare you into someone who can walk in everything He has planned for your life.

It is critical you know the season God has you in. Oftentimes, hardship and difficulty do not mean you are off course but simply that He is preparing you for greatness. ***Seasons of comfort seldom transform you into who God desires you to be.***

CHAPTER 4

REALIGNMENT AND REDIRECTION

Often in life we lose direction and our alignment with God. Our alignment with God goes another way, during our journey in life. As believers, when we receive Christ into our lives, we have an alignment with God through Christ, this means that we love and fear Him and worship Him. We hate what He hates, love what He loves, and we are ready to do whatever He asks us to do.

Alas we sometimes miss it along the way and our alignment with God shifts and we are not in sync with Him anymore. We are not going in the same direction God is taking us to , we then decide to go in our own direction , we tend to do whatever we like although we still go to church every now and then, lifting “holy hands”, in fact, we are even workers in His vineyard. Deep down, we know within ourselves that we are no more in alignment with God.

You see, God is a loving, merciful and gracious God. He has a purpose for our lives, and He would allow certain things to happen to us to realign and redirect us back to His purpose and plans for our lives. With my wilderness experience and process, I strongly believe God used it to realign and redirect me to Him and His purpose and plans for my life.

There is nothing you need that God cannot do. But you need to share in His desires and His goal is to get you to a place where you and He will be on this same page, in alignment.

Let me share my personal story with you to buttress this realignment and redirection of the process stage of our lives. By the grace and mercies of God, I receive Christ into my life as my Lord and Saviour on July 10th, 1996, which means I got born again and became part of the family of God.

God's 'No' is a not a rejection. It is a redirection

While in Nigeria, before I relocated to the United Kingdom, I was really on fire for God and serving Him in different capacity with tangible exploits and results. During my undergraduate days, I was a member of Nigerian Fellowship of Evangelical Students (NIFES), Federal Polytechnic, Offa Kwara State.

Where I was discipled and taught Biblical foundational doctrines, and this indeed helped me in living my Christian faith while on campus as a student. While at home I was a dedicated worker at RCCG Livingstone Parish, the local assembly I worshipped at then.

After the completion of my Higher National Diploma (HND) in Computer Science, and as the culture in Nigeria, we are expected to serve our nation through a scheme known as National Youth Service Corps (NYSC) where students upon graduation will be posted to different part of the country aside from your state of origin and the location of the school you had graduated from.

So, for me, I completed my education in the South West of the country and for my service year, I was posted to the South-South, Akwa Ibom State, to be precise.

After spending six weeks at the orientation camp, I was then sent to the place of my primary assignment, a town known as Eket under Eket Local Government as teacher in a secondary school known as Afaha Eket Government

School, to teach and educate the students on how to use computer.

While at the orientation camp , I lived my Christian faith , did the work of an evangelist and became a member of Nigerian Christian Corpers Fellowship (NCCF) , Word-based , Spirit filled and Holy Ghost energised fellowship that is committed to disciple Graduates in their walk with the Lord.

I am forever grateful that I was part of this fellowship throughout my service year. I continued to serve the Lord greatly with all my strength, spirit, soul, and body. I became the Zonal Liaison Officer (ZLO) serving alongside the Zonal Coordinator and Assistant Zonal Coordinator (Pastor (Mrs.) Abimbola Arawande) who is a very close friend and Kingdom partner till today as we both reside here in the UK. I also held the position of President of the NYSC Charity Club where my leadership skill was developed and sharpened.

As zonal executives, our responsibilities were to cater for the spiritual needs and welfare of the corps members in the six local governments under our zone. We were also required to organise evangelistic events and crusades to reach out to our host-community and establish the Kingdom of God by sharing the love of Jesus.

With these responsibilities and being the ZLO, I travelled every now and then. In fact, most of the responsibility was on me as I had a flexible time compared to the Zonal Coordinator. To the glory of God, we had a glorious and fantastic testimonies as God used us greatly and did miraculous things through us. Our rural rugged evangelism was backed by the power of God amidst the power of darkness in the village of IKWE.

One of our memorable and remarkable achievements and accomplishments was the Christian Film we acted and produced. The film was launched and sold to other corps members, churches, and our host community. It was indeed a glorious service year. Our host-community became our testimony and we could see how God transformed their lives as well as other corps member through the preaching of the gospel and we are forever grateful to God.

After my service year, I returned home to my parents and within two months I got a job as a System Engineer in a Computer Firm and I was very grateful to God. I continued serving the Lord at my local Church (RCCG, Livingstone Parish) in various capacities, expressing my gifts and calling as a Sunday School Teacher, Bible Study Teacher, Prayer Warrior, House Fellowship Leader and as well as an Usher.

This continued until 2004 when I relocated to the UK. You see, UK was not in the list of the countries I would have travelled to – US, Canada and Ireland were the countries I had in mind. Travelling out of Nigeria was not a do or die affair for me, though I would attend various education seminars from different Universities from the UK, US, Canada, and Ireland. I remember then that Newfoundland University in Canada gave me an unconditional admission which I needed to pay about 20% of the tuition fees. Unfortunately, I could not afford it and the relationship between myself and my father was not cordial anymore because he married another woman after my mother. Story for another day.

I forgot about travelling abroad and went ahead and enrolled for my Post Graduate Diploma (PGD) in Marketing so has to do my Masters in Business Administration (MBA). By the end of 2003 I had completed my PGD and in the middle of 2004 I submitted my application for the MBA. A close friend of mine who turned family had some older guys he was friendly with. So, one of them asked for favour from me, through my friend. My friend spoke to me about it and I agreed to be of help.

Eventually, he travelled to the UK and upon his return, he asked if I would like to travel to the UK and immediately, I replied with a 'yes', although UK was not in my plan. I prayed about it and it was settled. We proceeded with the arrangements and as God would have it, the visa was granted. You see ignorantly, I did not find out more information about education, working and living in UK but because it was an opportunity that came, I felt I needed to maximise it.

I remember asking him and he told me that there are various ways things are done in UK. He further said that the visiting visa was for me to gain entrance into the UK and once in, I would have to find a way to get my stay and live legally.

He continued by telling me I would need to use a fake document to work until I found a way to regularise my stay. On hearing this, I was perplexed and saddened knowing that I was about to go against Godly principles, also my parents and siblings were already aware, and they were all excited and happy for me. In fact, my father paid part of my travel ticket when I was leaving.

December 5th, 2004, I arrived in the UK, got a taxi from Heathrow airport to my sister's mother-in-law's house in Manor Park, East London. I was given a pleasant welcome and she called my sister to notify her of my safe arrival. I immediately acclimatised to my new environment, reached out to few friends that we lived in the same neighbourhood together, back in Nigeria.

My fake documents arrived, and I began my job hunting without no success. End of February, I got a job, guess what the job was? A street sweeper through a recruitment agency (Elite Agency), London Road in Barking, East London. Sweeping the streets of Stratford Train Station in East London. Prior to this,

I had submitted various applications either as a support worker or security man of nothing less than thirty applications and all to no avail. I did the street sweeping for about two weeks until one day when my sister's mother-in-law gave me a call and said she was not happy with the kind of job I was doing, so upon hearing this I had to quit the job.

February / March 2005, I made some phone calls and then moved to Oxford. Within a week of arriving in Oxford, I got a job in McDonalds right in the City Centre. I then started saving some money to regularise my stay and got a vital information which was very helpful that I could apply as a student although I may need to return home and obtain a student visa and comeback as a student.

After about three months of working at McDonalds, I got a support worker job to achieve my goal. I then went to apply to different universities and two gave me an unconditional admission. With the admission letters, I was happy that I was in the right direction as my plan to regularise my stay was on track. And with the information given to me and what was going around, I had to send my passport back to Nigeria so as to renew my visiting visa to serve as a backup plan peradventure the student visa application would not be granted and I could then return to the UK with the visiting visa.

While I was making all these plans, I met a beautiful lady who is now my wife today. We started our relationship and in December 2005, in our absence, a traditional wedding was done on our behalf and by April 2006 we had our marriage blessing in the Church.

Prior to this, in August 2005 after I had sent my passport back home for the renewal of my visitor's visa , I got a call from my father saying that the visiting visa's renewal application had been refused and my previous visa had also been cancelled. However, I was advised to lodge an appeal. I was so devastated as it meant than I could not travel to Nigeria to obtain the student's visa to regularise my stay and I was not prepared to take the risk of appealing the decision.

Do not forget that all these while, my faith in God had now been questionable though I still attended Church and also was an usher in a local church in

Northampton where my wife and I relocated to, to start our relationship and build our family. I was perplexed and confused on what to do, prayer was the last thing on my mind as I thought there was no other way to regularise my stay. I concluded to working illegally until I figured out what to do, to provide for my wife and first daughter who arrived in late 2006.

Life continued until August 2009 when I began my wilderness and process stage which lasted for ten years. This incidence happened to be what God use for realignment and redirection in my life. I held on to my dream to having education in the UK, because of my thirst for information, I was able to change my job as a support worker and healthcare assistant to a more exciting and pleasant one.

April 2008, I got a job in the retail sector at Three UK Retail Ltd to be precise, I started working in a mobile phone store as a Sales Associates and within six months I was promoted to a Sales Specialist with the responsibilities of a key holder and next to the Assistant Manager. That same year, I got an admission to a University with the fake document to study Professional Diploma in Marketing, Chartered Marketing Institute (CMI) with the plan to secure a marketing position at the head office.

Four months into the course, I had to defer the course with plans of picking it up in the next academic year, because my wife was seriously ill, so I needed to be there for her and our child who also has a medical condition (Sickle Cell).

By June 2009, an internal vacancy was open in the store for the position of an assistant manager as the store manager was leaving and the assistant manager would become the store manager. The then assistant manager came to me and encouraged me to apply as I stood more chance to be offered the job due to my sales figure and track record in the store. I had the most conversion rate out all the ten members of staff we had in the store and I was the only black African. This was a great news and opportunity for me because before that time, I had been taking the responsibilities of the assistant manager.

You need to understand that God cannot be mocked and whatsoever a man soweth so shall he reap. During my time at the store, my alignment with God had shifted, I had no strong and intimate relationship with God anymore, although I was an usher at my local Church. I mixed with the wrong people and engaged in some shady things that increased my commission every month and sometimes my commission would exceed my monthly salary.

I was exposed to some fraudulent activities which I personally knew it was totally wrong and against the company policy. However, God will not leave us without a witness. You see God always gives us a warning signs and sometimes He would send people to warn us, for us to repent and turn our ways back to Him when He sees we are heading towards destruction. On so many occasions, God would use my wife to warn me as she was not comfortable with the shady activities

I was involved in, at my workplace. Instead of heeding to her words of advice, I was always reassuring her that there would be no problem.

These guys would come to the store to obtain mobile phone contracts and their target was high end phones. They would come to me straight and at first, I did not take notice of it as I was naïve and also my commission was my goal because for every sale you make or any contract that goes through you with high end phones, you would get a big commission. As a result, this makes my job a very competitive one.

After about two occasions, I noticed that these same people brought different debit or credit cards with different names. The people would come to purchase phones when cardholders are male, as this is in line with the company policy. When the card is registered as female, they would send a lady to come and meet me in the store and I would put the mobile phone contract through without thorough information collation because my motivation was to get the commissions.

July 2009, a black guy, and a lady walked into the store and I approached them and closed the sale. I carried out a credit check on the lady, it was declined, and she was asked to pay a deposit of £150 and after six months she will get her deposit back. So, they both left to have a think about it.

Two or three days after, the black guy walked into the store. He was not my regular guy and he came to me directly that they would love to have the mobile phone and I explained to him that I would need to carry out another credit check and he answered OK.

I remembered very well that I did ask him where the lady was, and he told me she quick had to get few things in Tesco as it was adjacent to our store and she would join us later. Because I had seen both of them together, I sat him down, re-run the credit check and it came as passed without any deposit. I should have waited for the lady to be there before I put the sales through. However, as

I mentioned earlier, my highest motivation was the juicy commission on those sales.

You see warnings signs were there, but I ignored them, I shut God out of my life. I was not in alignment and in sync with God anymore despite being an usher in the church.

I put a contract through in a lady's name and the lady was not present. It was totally against the company's policy and I would have to take a full responsibility of my negligent attitude. In retrospective, I should not have allowed him to leave the store until the lady returned from her shopping at Tesco. This is a guy I have never met before except the first time he came with the lady. I don't usually see him around and it was later I gathered information that they both live in a neighbouring town (Wellingborough).

About four to five weeks later, August 2009 to be precise, two policemen walked into the store. I spoke with them and they requested to check the CCTV. I informed the store manager. All along,

I never knew the police were at the store because of my negligence. I was informed thereafter. The manager made a call to the head office compliance and security department to get a permission. The police went through the CCTV and saw the recording of the customer and how the transaction transpired.

Apparently, this male customer and the lady had a fall out and he went ahead to take a phone contract on the lady's name without her consent. The lady reported the incidence to the police, and they came to the store to investigate the fraudulent act.

Two days after, the policemen came to the store again and asked for the contract's paperwork. After going through the documents, they notified the store manager of the need to do more investigation in order to investigate my involvement in it since the transaction was done in our store and I was the one that put it through. Immediately, the store manager notified the head office and I was suspended with immediate effect, requested to leave the store. I could not believe what had just happened.

As a result, I could not go home straight away to inform my wife who had warned me on many occasions. Rather I went to a friend's house to cool it off and to get my head straight. By 5.30pm I headed home as if I was coming from work and remembered telling my wife that I was off for the next two days as I needed to summon the courage to break the news to her and inform her of what had happened. After two days I eventually told her. She did not take it lightly with me. In fact, our marriage almost ended.

A week later, I received a letter from the head office for a disciplinary meeting and was also informed to bring a colleague and Union representative with me. August 18th, 2009, I went for the disciplinary hearing. Series of questions were asked and before that time, I had gone to God to ask for forgiveness and repented. So, I gave an honest answer to every question that I was asked. By Friday 28th of August, I received another letter about the outcome of the hearing. I was dismissed with immediate effect!

Hoping that was the end of the whole ordeal, and at least I could move on with my life, only for the police to turn up at my doorstep on Thursday the 3rd September 2009. I was arrested and taken to the station for questioning. You see, I was so confident because I thought I had nothing I was hiding and would be returning home that same day. Oblivious to police investigations, that I would not be back home for the next four months.

Here is what happened- after the police have interviewed me to establish if I was an accomplice with this male customer, and apparently, thcy had been looking for him for some time. The lady he came with, was his girlfriend. He took her credit card without her consent to obtain the mobile phone and after some weeks, they fell out and later the bill came to her house. She was surprised about a mobile phone bill in her name and she went to report it to the police. The police rang store and came later to check our CCTV and established the fact that the guy was in the store.

They interviewed me and I gave them my own side of the story and was honest with them about my negligence in going against the company policy.

After about forty-five minutes of questioning, they concluded that they would have to release me as it seems to them that I was not an accomplice to the guy and no prior relationship between us. Abruptly, one of the cops asked me about my immigration status - if I was in the UK legally or illegally.

I then said, “no comment”. So, they went back to the store and obtained the document I submitted when I applied for the job and ran a check on it with the Home Office (Immigration Department) and obviously it would not be genuine. It was at this point that they arrested and charged me for obtaining an employment with a false document.

I was locked up that day. The next day, Friday 4th September, I was taken to the magistrate court in Kettering. On getting to the magistrate court, there were four judges and they concluded that the case should be taken to the Crown Court as it was against the Secretary of State and I should be remanded in the prison until the Crown Court finds a date for me to appear in court.

What had just happened? My whole world collapsed! Me, in prison! I wept and cried like a child on that day. So, I was taken to Her Majesty Prison (HMP Woodhill) in Milton Keynes where I spent the next four months. On getting to the prison, I could remember vividly my first night, the Word of the Lord came expressly to me which was a scripture in Job 22 vs 23 and it says *"If thou return to the Almighty, thou shalt be built up, thou shalt put away iniquity far from thy tabernacles"*

This was then repeated to me for another two nights making it three nights. On the third night which was on Monday 7th, I returned to my

Maker and Creator. *The grace of God is a radical agent that transforms us from inside out.*

My court date at the Crown Court was fixed however was postponed three times. I had dressed up and ready to be moved to court only for me to be informed that there was no Judge available.

On Tuesday 24th, November 2009, I appeared in court. You see, God gave me favour in the sight of the Judge, he sentenced me for five months including the time I had spent on remand. By the time it was calculated, my sentence finished on that very day.

Lest I forget, around October 2009, by the help of one of my uncles, my wife had applied to regularise my stay at the Home Office. Due to this, when my sentence came to an end, the Home Office refused to release me until my bail was granted so I was released from the Prison on Friday 18th, December 2009.

I share this story to say this, that my wilderness experience while in the prison was an avenue for God to redirect me and realign me back to His purpose and plan for my life.

The next ten years, after I was released from the prison, had been a wonderful and glorious time of fellowship with the Lord. While in the prison, I was mindful of who to associate myself with. I studied, read, and meditated upon God's Word. I evangelised and prayed with other prisoners. Most importantly, I discovered my purpose and my calling.

My life is not for me to determine, my life is for me to discover.

By His grace and mercy, I discovered my life and purpose. God gave me specific instructions and assignment to be carried out. Today I know my direction and where my alignment is because God realigned and redirected me through my wilderness experience.

A man without direction will take every direction……Get a direction. If you have lost it, allow Him to redirect you.

You see, after I returned home and had returned to the Lord according to His Word, He started building me up. With my bail conditions, I was restricted from working for ten years and had to report at the immigration report Centre which lasted for ten years too.

So many words of advice were given to me - "don't go to report, you would be deported", "move away to another part of the UK, you cannot sit and not work in this country, how would you survive?" etc. . From a human point of view, all these words of advice are good, but they are not right in the eyes of God and because the Lord had given me a sure Word, I held on to it.

The next ten years, I reported at the immigration reporting centre every two weeks. It later changed to monthly and eventually every six months. Within that ten years, I could not work, I had no source of income and I was literally living on the favour of God with my wife and three children.

The most important thing was that I realigned myself with God's plan and purpose for my life. I was redirected to the path of righteousness through my wilderness experience. You might be thinking of how I survived it. All I can mention is that His grace was sufficient for me.

There were many tempting times to work illegally but I could not; at times I would try to take a wrong step but He would whisper to me that His grace is not available for me if I tried working again illegally. Many times, in tears, I would go back and pray and ask for God's strength to carry on.

Satan has a strategy to stop you from completing journey into destiny and fulfilling your purpose. The good news is that God has an unchangeable strategy to keep you on track.

By His grace and mercy, December 7th, 2013, I was officially and publicly ordained into ministry and today I am an ordained Pastor and Evangelist to the Body of Christ. Founder of Men's Empowerment Network (MEN), *Acting International Coordinator* – Flaming Sword Ministries UK and the Resident Pastor of God's City Assembly - Wolverhampton , host, and facilitator of Redefining Leadership Series - a personal and leadership transformation seminar.

To crown it all, June 2019, after ten years of waiting on the Lord, I was granted legal stay to remain, live and work in the UK.

In chapter 10 I share the rewards for waiting on God.

Never allow the devil to use what you are going through to knock you out of your divine assignment.

CHAPTER 5

OPPORTUNITY AND OBEDIENCE

God has a wonderful way of disguising opportunities as problems. In whatever process or wilderness stage you are now, there are opportunities in them. In your pain, there is an opportunity that God wants you to maximise.

Waiting for a miracle or a breakthrough should not stop you from being productive with time.

Time is so precious that you cannot afford to waste it. Time is not money. Time is life, and life is measured in time. No matter what you are waiting on God for, you must decide to be productive with the time you have while awaiting the fulfilment of that promise. Do not lose your life at the expense of what you are waiting or trusting God for.

Where you find pain, you will always find opportunity – C.J Benjamin

The most important thing to know about anything in life is its purpose. Because if you do not know the purpose of a thing, you will abuse it. The waiting period is not a wasted time and not a time to be idle, you must learn how to be productive and maximize the opportunity in that waiting period, if not you will abuse that time of your waiting.

It might be a time for you to learn, unlearn and relearn new things, a time to grow in the Lord and a time to build relationships that would be useful when the promise is fulfilled.

You need to understand that you cannot afford to miss opportunities that are in that season of your life.

God has a wonderful way of disguising opportunities as problems.

God has always been in the business of disguising opportunities as problems. Take Joseph for example, when he was in the prison, he maximised and converted the problem he was in, as an opportunity to express his gift of interpretation of dreams.

Genesis 39 vs 22 says ***"And the keeper of the prison committed to Joseph's hand all the prisoners that were in the prison; and whatsoever they did, he was the doer"***

Imagine a prisoner in charge of all other prisoners, Joseph was not bothered about his pain but the opportunities in that pain was what was motivating him. He also interpreted the baker and butler's dream in Chapter 40 and in verse 14 it says ***"But think on me when it shall be well with thee, and shew kindness, I pray thee, unto me, and make mention of me unto Pharaoh, and bring me out of this house:"***

Although the chief butler forgot Joseph when Pharaoh restored him unto his butlership post, agai**n.** What I am saying here is that, in the time of your pain or waiting for a breakthrough, ***you*** need to pray that the Lord should open your eyes to the opportunity that lies in that pain?

Interestingly in Chapter 41, Pharaoh now had a dream, and no one could interpret the dream, neither could the magicians. That was the moment the chief butler remembered his relationship and encounter with Joseph, and how Joseph interpreted everyone's dream in the prison, and how they all came to pass.

Verse 14 then says "***Then Pharaoh sent and called Joseph, and they brought him hastily out of the dungeon: and he shaved himself, and changed his raiment, and came in unto***

Pharaoh" This opportunity Joseph had been praying for now presented itself and Joseph had only one thing- to maximise it.

You need to package yourself for where you are going not where you are now or where you have been.

Opportunity is defined as a time or set of circumstances that make it possible to do something. I believe Joseph must have known about this definition, there was a set of circumstances which made it possible for him to do something.

In life no matter what your level of education, the career pathway you follow, the people you surround or that surround you, you need opportunity, time and chance for things to happen in your life. The problem however is that opportunity, time, and chance do not announce themselves. Even when they arrive, these factors do not announce "we are here".

You may have heard this before "look around you, there are opportunities everywhere". That might be true in most cases, but when you are not conscious of it, you will not be aware. Being conscious demands being deliberate and being prepared; and this takes effort.

When opportunity comes, it will be too late to begin to prepare; and opportunity may be lost and never regained. That is why you must live "ready" and seize the moment. When opportunity meets preparation, success is inevitable. If you miss the preparation stage, opportunities will elude you.

While I was in my pain, waiting for a breakthrough for my immigration matter to be resolved, I had to look and create an opportunity for what I could invest my time in. I did numerous courses especially in leadership development, attended seminars and conferences both spiritual and career-wise. I also develop and sharpened my public speaking skills. I was preparing myself for any opportunity that might come my way.

It paid off for me and today apart from being a Pastor, I'm also a Certified Life Coach, Personal & Leadership Development Coach, A Trainer & Facilitator and Mentor, Change Strategist, Culture Catalyst, Transformational Speaker and as well as a Management Board Member of ISI PLUS, a charity youth organisation, Member of Wolverhampton Inclusion Board. More so, I organise a Men2Men Breakfast Meeting where men from different walks of life gather to be empowered and equipped for national transformation and global impact.

When you are in a storm or going through pain, God is writing a new chapter in your life that is a testimony.

Leonard Ravenhill (1907 – 1994) said ***"The opportunity of a lifetime must be seized within the lifetime of the opportunity"*** God indeed wrote a new chapter in my life which is now a testimony. Today, I speak, train, and educate others, especially in personal and leadership development. I also organise a personal and leadership development seminar tagged Redefining Leadership Series, which is totally free to attend. All these could happen because I seized the opportunity in my pain, rather than working illegally, I invested in my time. I used my time wisely.

Dr Olumuyiwa Olumoroti in his book - T.O.A.S.T. – A CONSCIOUS THINKING APPROACH, wrote about the seven kind of opportunities and what to do with them, also seven levels of opportunities.

The **seven kinds of opportunities and what to do with them** are

1) Opportunities that you possess – cherish them.
2) Opportunities given to you – utilise them in time.
3) Opportunities that you stumble upon – take advantage of them.

4) Opportunities that you are looking for – be optimistic and patient.
5) Opportunities that are looking for you – discern them.
6) Opportunities that you see in others – position yourself.
7) Opportunities that you create – be strategic and precise.

He went further to rank these seven opportunities and mentioned you can rank them in order of your being in control and their ability to give maximum results. Let us see a summary of these seven levels of opportunities.

1. **OPPORTUNITIES THAT YOU POSSESS** – if you are endowed or possess any tangible or intangible attributes, cherish them and be grateful as you did not do anything to deserve or possess them. It may be that you are born into wealthy family, a prosperous nation or with a gift of the voice of an angel or dancing or wisdom or any other thing for that matter. Cherish them, use

them for positive actions and do not let them go to waste.

2. **OPPORTUNITIES GIVEN TO YOU** – Every moment in life, men and women, boys and girls, are given opportunities to be or do something. It is important that those opportunities are not taken for granted. Such opportunities should be utilised in good time to improve self and others; and to make positive impact. Otherwise the opportunities may be passed on to others who are willing to make use of them. When you are given an opportunity, time is of essence.

3. **OPPORTUNITIES THAT YOU STUMBLE UPON** – If you stumble upon good (relevant) opportunity, take advantage of it. Grab it, do not let it go. There may be need for you to negotiate and partner with others to take maximum advantage of the opportunity that you stumble upon. Do not be silly or play/act ignorant. ***"Even if you do not feel ready, think***

of what you can do to be able to make use of the opportunity."

4. **OPPORTUNITIES THAT YOU ARE LOOKING FOR** – You need to be proactive, optimistic, and patient if you are looking for certain opportunities. Having good mentors have taught us that even while you are looking for an opportunity, you really must be prepared. You do not just sit and do nothing. You must invest in what you are looking for. The truth is this: many hundreds (or thousands) are looking for the same kind of opportunities, all over the world.

5. **OPPORTUNITIES THAT ARE LOOKING FOR YOU** – Discernment is key when it comes to an opportunity or opportunities that are looking for you. You have to discern them. When an opportunity is looking for you, you must have something to offer.

6. **OPPORTUNITIES THAT YOU SEE IN OTHERS** – If you see an opportunity in another person, do not be shy or timid about

exploring it. Position yourself and find the common good. If you do not, others will take advantage of the same opportunity. The most important thing is to look for how the opportunity will benefit you and the other person.

7. **OPPORTUNITIES THAT YOU CREATE.** – This is the highest level of opportunity that anyone could have – when you create one. However, you must be careful to be strategic and definite in what you are creating, otherwise you could waste a lot of time and effort. The opportunity that you create must necessarily meet a need. You must be strategic and precise. Wise people create opportunities instead of waiting to meet some. The best way to prepare for an opportunity is by creating it. Ask yourself some serious questions: have you spotted something, or have you noticed something strange today? What have you done about it? One of the most beneficial ways of creating opportunities for yourself is to go and help people or study at the University of Life in whatever country you may live.

You see the number seven – opportunities you create- was what Joseph did, he created opportunities for himself while he was in the prison by interpreting other prisoners' dreams including the chief butler's dream. I did the same while I was in my wilderness, I had to create an opportunity for myself rather than just sitting idle. Imagine if I did not do that, I would have just sat down idle for ten years doing nothing all because I was waiting on God for a breakthrough.

Be a man or woman of wisdom – create opportunities

Thomas Edison said, "The *reason why most people do not recognise an opportunity when they meet it is because it usually goes around wearing overalls and looking like hard work."*

Dr Muyiwa continued in his book – *"It is however important to recognise these opportunities for what they are. Opportunities are like windows – they do not stay open forever."* You must be prepared for every opportunity that you expect or the one that may come your way. Wise people do not wait for opportunities; they create them. These people look for where to invest their resources and pursue their dreams passionately.

Do not wait for things to be perfect, begin to work on what you have and where you are now. The question is "How do you spot an opportunity?"

Dr Muyiwa, in the same book, mentioned few of them. Let us look at them:

- Keep your eyes open.
- Act fast. ***Where there is a problem, a challenge or a need, there is an opportunity.***
- Ask the right questions: "Is there a need here? Can I make it better or faster or less expensive?
- Embrace what you are not used to; something might just be close by.
- Check the trends, think and focus.

- If someone knocks your idea off the perch, thank them instead of arguing.

Ways to maximise opportunities

1) Consider the seven levels of opportunities. Discern which ones pertain to you.
2) Consciously think about opportunities; they are everywhere and waiting to be grabbed.
3) Constantly look out for opportunities – sometimes they are like a moving cloud – they do not stay in the same direction.
4) Be sensitive to opportunities – they can come disguised as responsibilities. Also be careful; some are traps and not worth it.
5) Look for ways to maximise the opportunities.
6) Guard any opportunity that you have jealously and do not let them go to waste.
7) Ask which opportunity has the greatest chance success. Do not waste time on what appears to be good opportunity but yields very low return for your time and effort or investment.
8) Do something about the opportunities that present themselves to you. Do not think an

idea to death or wait for when everything is going to be perfect.

9) Never give up. If anything is proving too hard to crack, know that others might be feeling the same way too. You will certainly be at an advantage if you get there first. Also, seek help.
10) Learn from mistakes, particularly if you have missed an opportunity. Almost always, another opportunity is around the corner.

Reasons why people miss or misuse opportunities

- Failure to recognise opportunities.
- Lack of ambition, goals, or targets.
- Lack of preparation, capability, and capacity.
- Fear of failure, adverse consequences or of suffering.
- Concerns about being embarrassed, ridiculed, or rejected.
- The convenience of the 'comfort zone' and the lure of the familiar.

- Easier or easy alternatives, perfectionism and waiting for the ideal time.
- Negative mindset and focus on short-term gain.
- Lack of passion and self-confidence, and mistrust.
- Procrastination, complacency, or laziness.
- Other people's opinion and distraction. "What will people say?"
- Obstructive or hostile environment.

Abraham Graham Bell – inventor of the telephone said this:

"Nothing can change the past; we can only learn from it. If at any point in your life you miss an opportunity, ponder only for a little while and move on. When one door closes, another door opens. But we often look so long and regretfully upon the closed door, that we do not see the ones which open almost instantly for us, as that door closes."

OBEDIENCE

Hebrews 5 vs 8 says *"Though he were a Son, yet learned he obedience by the things which he suffered:"*

This is talking about Jesus our Saviour, through His sufferings, He learnt obedience. In other words, God wants us to learn and be obedient even through the things we suffer or the pain we are going through. The obedience he learned was a submission to undergo great, hard, and terrible things, accompanied with patience under them and faith for deliverance from them.

He endured unpleasant experiences as suffering was required to learn obedience. It implies enduring a challenging process that transforms the sufferer. Jesus chose to endure an unpleasant, challenging process because it was the will of His Father for His brief time on earth. After that process Jesus had been made perfect. Perfect here means complete as in finishing a full course of training or education. In Jesus' case, He finished an altogether righteous human life and had complete understanding of human frailty and suffering. It was Christ's total human obedience, coming through extreme suffering, that qualifies Him to be our eternal High Priest, ***"now crowned with glory and honour because he suffered death – vs 9***

As much as we hate being in the wilderness- being in difficult times, being physically weakened, being spiritually stretched, being emotionally drained- these are times that God uses to refine, change, remove elements of pride and self-sufficiency and teaches us to depend on Him.

Why does God allow this? He allows it so as not to harm us but to keep us from destroying ourselves in our own pride. So that we would not live miserable life but ultimately have an abundant life. So that we will not live in discouragement but to give us a hope and a future. ***(Jeremiah 29 vs 11).***

Your current obedience is what qualifies you for your next instruction.

You see, believe it or not, God's number one priority is not to make you happy, fulfilled or to have everything go your way. His primary agenda for your life is to make you like His Son.

Obedience to God is the true demonstration of our trust in Him to do what He has said. It begins in holding fast to saying and doing the same thing God is saying about our situation. It is the key to fulfilment of God's promises in our lives.

CHAPTER 6

COURAGE AND COMMITMENT

Joshua 1: 6 says *"Be strong and of a good courage: for unto this people shalt thou divide for an inheritance the land, which I sware unto their fathers to give them...*

One of the qualities you need to have or develop in your wilderness or process period is courage and commitment. You must understand the need to be courageous during your pain and hard times while you are awaiting a breakthrough. Your commitment to the process is very essential to coming out better after the process has ended.

Courage, they say, ***is not the absence of fear, but the decision to go ahead despite the fear.***

Francis Bob Alonge, in his book – "**The Making of a Chosen Vessel**, said that we all need courage. A chosen vessel must always be a person of courage. Courage is not just being bold and fearless. It is the ability to still do the right thing even when fear surrounds you. Please note that there is a huge difference between courage and fearlessness. Fearlessness is synonymous with naivety and simple mindedness.

Courage is what David had when he ran towards Goliath instead of running away from him. The trick is to put a smile on your face, look at the devil eyeball to eyeball and do what you know is the right thing to do. Stand on God's Word to have peace of mind. Call his bluff, do what you must do, and God will honour you. Do not think for one moment that David's heart was not pounding when he faced Goliath. A chose person must have courage."

The difference between interest & commitment: interest says count me in as long as it is convenient. Commitment says I am in it for the long haul and accept no excuses… only results.

You need to understand that you are a chosen person, a royal priesthood, and a peculiar person. God has chosen you for such a time as this but that does not mean challenges or trials will not come your way. You must be courageous during pain, challenges and wilderness you are in now.

He went ahead in the book, to explain how we can receive courage.

Deuteronomy 31 vs 6 "*Be strong and of a good courage, fear not, nor be afraid of them: for the LORD thy God, he it is that doth go with thee; he will not fail thee, nor forsake thee.*"

"The more conscious we are of the capacity of God and His involvement in a situation, the more courageous we become in that situation. True courage is not rooted in our own ability, but in the ability of God. Courage happens when we look not to our own strength or the complexity of the situation, but God's might and His promise and commission instead. Courage is produced by transcendent thinking. If we magnify the challenges, we minimise our consciousness of the ability and grace of God available to us. It is a substitution of focus that produces courage. God is only prayer away and prayer turns our gaze in His direction. If you begin to feel like been swept off your feet, get on your knees."

Courage and confidence also come when we obey God.

God's promise will usually follow His instructions. He pays for what He orders. He stands behind anyone He has sent. He watches over His Word to perform it.

Courage is not having the strength to go on. It is going on when you do not have the strength.

COMMITMENT

A willingness to give your time and energy to something that you believe in, or a promise or firm decision to do something:

As God is always committed to do whatsoever, He has promised us, so you also need to be committed to the process He is taking you through.

You must give your time and energy to the belief you have in God, that what He had promised to do, He will surely bring it performance. In other words, you must be convinced without any iota of doubt that faithful is He who has promised. (Hebrews 10: 23)

One of the most important lessons I have learnt as a life coach is that becoming successful at anything requires commitment. There will be many obstacles on the path to accomplishing a worthwhile goal. When those obstacles appear, it is easy to lose the belief and thus the motivation to continue the same path.

"It was character that got us out of bed, commitment that moved us into action, and discipline that enabled us to follow through." – Zig Ziglar.

Commitment is what will move you into action, action to study, read and meditate of the Word of God, to be joyful, praise and worship even amid your challenges.

The only way you will enjoy a long-term relationship with someone is if you are committed to that relationship. The only way you will enjoy a successful career is if you are committed to it. The only way you will enjoy life's journey is if you are committed to making the best of it and living life to its fullest.

For you to enjoy your relationship with God in the midst of your pain, is to be committed to God.

Also, for you to enjoy the journey and your process time, is to make a commitment of making the best of it and live your life to its fullest.

During my ten years of waiting for my breakthrough, God gave me the grace to be committed to the process and to make best use of that time and I lived life to its fullest. I attended Church services as usual, visited friends and families, spoke in conferences, trained, empowered others, and attended social gatherings.

Commitments are powerful because they influence how you think, sound, and act. Unlike a half-hearted hope or 'best shot,' making a commitment means that you try harder, you look for solutions when faced with obstacles, you do not consider quitting as an option, and you do not look back.

In addition, a meaningful commitment gives you a script for how to handle things when times get tough. Make no mistake, everyone feels like quitting at one time or another. Unfortunately, most people quit when they feel like quitting, which is why they seldom succeed at anything.

Whether it is a relationship or marriage, job or career venture, fitness or health, or a personal improvement goal, the temptation to give up will arise. The key is to anticipate it and make yourself a promise that the feeling of wanting to quit will not overpower your commitment.

Commitment is a decision to stick with a project, idea, relationship, or goal – even when it is not easy

When things are difficult and seems overwhelming, commitment is needed. You cannot be committed only when things are easy, if you do, then you are living a mediocre life without taking any responsibility.

You always have two choices: your commitment versus your fear.

CHAPTER 7

EXPECTATION AND ENDURANCE

Proverbs 23 vs 18 says *''For surely there is an end; and thine expectation shall not be cut off.''*

You need to understand that everything that has a beginning also has an end. You must be expectant of the end of your wilderness and pain, that one day it will surely come to an end. Expectation is very important in our walk with God. Without it, we will remain hopeless. It is what gives us the energy and the drive not to give up during our trials.

Your expectation must be only from the Lord as Psalm 62: 5 says *"My soul, wait thou only upon God; for my expectation is from him."* Your waiting must be on God as only Him can do that which you are trusting Him for - that breakthrough and miracle.

Expectation **-** *A strong belief that something will happen or be the case, in the future.*

When you expect greatness, then you will receive greatness. It is not new-age thought. It is not a matter of luck. It is a matter of linking your faith with God's word.

Expecting greatness however is easier said than done. It is easy to expect greatness when greatness is going on all around you. But when the going gets tough, and the light at the end of the tunnel is getting dimmer and dimmer, expecting greatness becomes much more difficult.

Expectation is the mother of manifestation.

Expecting greatness is difficult. Ultimately because it requires us to have faith, something we Christians understand too well. Faith means that above reason, above obstacles, above your own senses, you choose to follow the path before you. Faith is doing something despite the chance of failure. Faith is what happens when the world is saying "no" and God is saying "yes"

Expect greatness even when the reality points to something otherwise. Expect everything to work out in the way that God has decided because they always do. Understand that while you and I make plans, God's plans are already falling into place. You must believe in better things and understand that even if they do not come to fruition with your plans, that they will, eventually.

Possibly, you are struggling financially, perhaps, you are having relationship issues, maybe your health or the health of your loved ones are not as you would desire, I encourage you - if you are still here, and you woke up this morning and are reading these words, then God is not done with you just yet! It is only over when God says so!

You cannot allow the weight of the ordeal to ruin your expectations of God's promises. Great expectations will lead to fruition, but negative expectations will lead only to failure. Whether you are expecting a feast or a famine, you will surely realise it. If you believe it, you can achieve it. Much of life is your mindset; you can have a positive mindset or a negative mindset.

The choice is yours. If you are having a difficult time, then have expectations for a metamorphosis!

In Proverbs 10:28, it says *that the hope of the righteous will bring you joy, but the expectation of the wicked will only perish.*

Expect growth over stagnation. Expect happiness over depression. Expect life over death. To have great expectations is not to pretend to be ignorant of obstacles or issues that you will face. It is not an absence of problems; it is the willingness to view the bigger picture despite your obstacles. Moses had issues.

He stuttered. He lacked confidence. When God was before him, telling him of the plans that He had for Moses, Moses still felt inadequate. Yet, with all these problems and his setbacks, he went on to lead the Israelites to freedom.

Moses might not have believed in himself. He might not have had great expectations originally, but when God called on him, he gained some great expectations! He had great expectations for the plans that God had called on him to do!

Against all his senses, Moses continued to have faith. Imagine having the fortitude that Moses had. Despite whatever the past has brought to you, despite your current circumstances, despite your problems, choose to have great expectations for the future.

To have great expectations, you need to have great goals. When God says something to you, make sure you record it because your spiritual enemy is an expert at stealing the seeds of truth that God wants to plant. The very act of putting your goals on the page or screen produces a testimony. It seals a memory, and it helps to hold you accountable for your goals. Record the goals that God instils in your heart.

To have great expectations is to understand that the floodgates of the LORD'S blessings and favour have been opened! Action is needed to bring our vision to fruition, but expectation is what is needed to get our vision off the ground in the first place! Expectation is needed for lift-off and action keeps our vision in the air. Consistency, dedication, discipline, and perseverance will carry us to our destination!

You are **ready!**
You are **purposed!**
You are **prepared!**

I believe that too many of us are addicted to this feeling called "ready." We are dependent on things happening at the "right time" or being "prepared" but the great men and women that God worked through are not people who had their own plan.

Instead, they worked with God's plan for themselves. Noah was told to build a boat where there was no water! David fought and killed a giant with no armour, just a sling and a stone. Moses was told to find water held within a rock!

So many people miss moments because of their need to "be ready." They let the fear of rejection, the fear of humiliation, and the fear of failure make their decisions for them. Do not wait for the perfect time, because you will never have it all figured out. Set out to reach your goals, and see your great expectations come to fruition.

ENDURING THROUGH SUFFERING

Most believers are familiar with the story of Joseph. He was cruelly sold into slavery by his brothers because of their envy. He was also unfairly imprisoned for doing what was right. Then he was forgotten by someone he helped in prison. In the end, the Lord elevated him to a high position in the foreign land where he was initially living as a slave and prisoner. Later, his brothers came to purchase food from him, and they did not recognise him.

He made himself known to them and then he said this in Genesis 45:5-8:

"And now, do not be distressed and do not be angry with yourselves for selling me here, because it was to save lives that God sent me ahead of you. For two years now there has been famine in the land, and for the next five years there will be no ploughing and reaping. But God sent me ahead of you to preserve for you a remnant on earth and to save your lives by a great deliverance. So then, it was not you who sent me here, but God. He made me father to

Pharaoh, lord of his entire household and ruler of all Egypt."

We read nearly the same statement by Joseph years later in Genesis 50:19-21. Joseph recognised God's hand at work through all the injustice, defamation, suffering and separation from his family and homeland. He did not harbour anger or bitterness against the people who were God's instruments in all those difficulties.

His focus was on doing God's work and pursuing God's purposes, whether he was a slave or in prison or in a position of great power and influence. He trusted God and was content to play whatever role God had for him and trust His goodness and timing, no matter the personal cost. May we learn to do the same.

Psalm 66:10-12 is an illustration of how Joseph handled and endured his suffering. *"For you, God, tested us; you refined us like silver. You brought us into prison and laid burdens on our backs. You let people ride over our heads; we went through fire and water, but you brought us to a place of abundance."*

Here the psalmist recognises how God is at work in, and through his suffering. He also recognises God's purposes. In this case, God's purposes were to test and refine the psalmist. The means was a variety of difficulties- imprisonment, hard labour, subjugation, and figuratively, fire and flood.

Again, there is a recognition of God's complete authority, wisdom and goodness through tremendous pain and suffering. There is trust in the Lord to bring His people through difficulties in the end and give them reward and comfort. For some, that reward and comfort may well be delayed until eternity, but the Lord is trustworthy. We can trust Him to do what is right and best.

Sometimes, our suffering is because of our own foolish decision, in my own case I made some foolish decisions. Lamentations 3:1-57 reminds us that at times, suffering comes because of our own sin, and God's way of punishing and correcting us:

"I will remember them, and my soul is downcast within me. 21 Yet this I call to mind and therefore I have hope: 22 Because of the LORD's great love we are not consumed, for his compassions never fail. 23 They are new every morning; great is your faithfulness. 24 I say to myself, "The LORD is my portion; therefore I will wait for him." 25 The LORD is good to those whose hope is in him, to the one who seeks him; 26 it is good to wait quietly for the salvation of the LORD. 27 It is good for a man to bear the yoke while he is young. 28 Let him sit alone in silence, for the LORD has laid it on him. 29 Let him bury his face in the dust— there may yet be hope. 30 Let him offer his cheek to one who would strike him, and let him be filled with disgrace. 31 For no one is cast off by the Lord forever. 32 Though he brings grief, he will show compassion, so great is his unfailing love. ..... 39 Why should the living

complain when punished for their sins? 40 Let us examine our ways and test them, and let us return to the LORD. 41 Let us lift up our hearts and our hands to God in heaven, ... 55 I called on your name, LORD, from the depths of the pit. 56 You heard my plea: "Do not close your ears to my cry for relief." 57 You came near when I called you, and you said, "Do not fear."

Even when the calamities that come upon us are due to our own sinfulness, Jeremiah recognises and mentions that God's goodness and mercy are in view. Despite our sinfulness, the Lord is acting for our own good. This is highlighted in verses 21-25 and 31-36.

Jeremiah gives helpful guidance on how we are to respond in such situations. Note all the instructions he gives in the passage. In summary, we are to repent and believe. We are to submit to God's ways and trust Him to know what is right and to do it. We are to devote ourselves to His path and trust His timing. We are to call on Him and do not fear.

Let us be ready to do His will, even when it means sacrifice and suffering. It is precisely our willingness to do so that shows everyone around us a measure of God's greatness, goodness, and worthiness. He is worth suffering for. We will have an eternity to dance without sacrifice or suffering. God is taking us somewhere. He is leading us to a greater and brighter path. However, it takes seeing and knowing where, to be able to endure where we are, what we are going through, and will go through.

CHAPTER 8

SUBMISSION AND SURRENDER

Mark 14: 36 says *"And he said, Abba, Father, all things are possible unto thee; take away this cup from me: nevertheless, not what I will, but what thou wilt."*

Luke 22: *"Father, if you are willing, take this cup from me; yet not my will, but yours be done." (NIV)*

Jesus was about to undergo the most difficult struggle of his life: the crucifixion. Not only was Christ facing one of the most painful and disgraceful punishments—death on a cross. He was dreading something even worse. Jesus would be forsaken by the Father (Matthew 27:46) as he took on sin and death for us:

For God made Christ, who never sinned, to be the offering for our sin, so that we could be made right with God through Christ. (2 Corinthians 5:21 NLT)

When we want something desperately, choosing God's will over our own is not an easy feat. God the Son understands better than anyone just how difficult this choice could be. When Jesus called us to follow him, he called us to learn obedience through suffering, just as he did.

"Even though Jesus was God's Son, he learned obedience from the things he suffered. In this way, God qualified him as a perfect High Priest,

and he became the source of eternal salvation for all those who obey him." (Hebrews 5:8–9 NLT)

Above all else, we must learn how to bring our will into submission and obedience of the will of God on a daily and practical basis.

If we truly trust God, we will have the strength to let go of our wants and passions, and believe that His will is perfect, right, and the *very best thing* for us.

Submit to God and trust him.
The will of God for your life is simply that you submit yourself to Him each day and say - *"Father, Your will for today is mine. Your pleasure for today is mine. Your work for today is mine. I trust You to be God. You lead me today and I will follow."* In your trying times, there is a need to submit to the will of God, not your own will. The will of God, for instance, might take four or five years to bring the promise to pass.

Submitting to His will, no matter how difficult it might be, will be for your own good.

Joseph submitted to the plan and purpose of God for his life, he could have escaped from the prison or leave Potiphar's house when the going got tougher. Instead, he submitted to the agenda of God for his life.

Carry the cross patiently, and with perfect submission; and in the end, it shall carry you.

Dwight L Moddy said *"Let God have your life; He can do more with it than you can"*

God wants to have your life in your trying and process period, so that He can do more with you than you can do for yourself. In the place of submission, you receive strength from above, not to give up.

"A man is not far from the gates of heaven when he is fully submissive to the Lord's - Charles Spurgeon

Heaven is where help comes from, when you submit fully to the will of God, the help you need to carry on will not be far-fetched. Never allow temptation of taking the short-cut, of bypassing the process God is taking you through. Inordinate desires commonly produce irregular endeavours. If our wishes are not kept in submission to God's providence, our pursuits will scarcely be kept under the restraints of His precepts.

Ability to resist temptation is directly proportionate to your submission to God.

We must choose to submit to God for the process of learning in order to grow spiritually. It is a process that begins at salvation, and ongoing with each choice that we make to submit ourselves to God. This process will continue until the Lord comes again or He calls us home.

The wonderful thing about this is that, as the Apostle Paul aptly states, *"But we all, with unveiled face beholding as in a mirror the glory of the Lord, are changed into the same image from glory to glory, even as by the spirit of the Lord" (2 Corinthians 3:18).*

God does not require us to submit because He is a tyrant, but because He is a loving Father and He knows what is best for us. The blessings and peace that we gain from humbly surrendering and submitting ourselves to Him daily are a gift of grace that nothing in this world can compare to. It is a rewarding process to surrender our own will to that of our Father's because Father's will is the most secure place.

Therefore, having a humble and submissive heart is a choice we make. This means that as born-again believers, we daily make a choice to submit ourselves to God for the work that the Holy Spirit does in us to ***"conform us to the image of Christ."*** God will use the situations of our lives to bring us the opportunity to submit to Him (Romans 8:28-29). We accept His grace and provision to walk in the Spirit and not after the manner of the old nature. That work is accomplished by choosing to apply ourselves to the Word of God and to learning about the provisions that God has made for us in Christ Jesus.

From the moment we are born again, we have all the provisions we need, in Christ, to become a mature believer, but we have to make the choice to learn about these provisions through studying of the Word and applying the provisions to our daily walk.

SURRENDER

Surrender is a battle term. It implies giving up all rights to the conqueror. When an opposing army surrenders, they lay down their arms, and the winners take control from then on. Surrendering to God can be likened to the analogy. God has a plan for our lives and surrendering to Him means we set aside our own plans and eagerly seek His. The good news is that God's plan for us is always in our best interest unlike our own plans that often lead to destruction. Our Lord is a wise and beneficent Victor; He conquers us to bless us.

There are different levels of surrender, all of which affect our relationship with God. Initial surrender to the drawing of the Holy Spirit leads to salvation. When we let go of our own attempts to earn God's favour and rely upon the finished work of Jesus Christ on our behalf, we become a child of God. But there are times of greater surrender during a Christian's life that brings deeper intimacy with God and greater power in service.

The more areas of our lives we surrender to Him, the more room there is for the filling of the Holy Spirit. When we are filled with the Holy Spirit, we exhibit traits of His character. The more we surrender to God, the more our old self-worshiping nature is replaced with one that resembles Christ.

Romans 6:13 says that God demands that we surrender the totality of our selves; He wants the whole, not a part: *"Do not offer any part of yourself to sin as an instrument of wickedness, but rather offer yourselves to God as those who have been brought from death to life; and offer every part of yourself to him as an instrument of righteousness."* Jesus said that His followers must deny themselves —another call to surrender.

The goal of the Christian life can be summed up by Galatians 2:20: *"I have been crucified with Christ. It is no longer I who live, but Christ who lives in me. And the life I now live in the flesh I live by faith in the Son of God, who loved me and gave himself for me."* Such a life of surrender is pleasing to God, it results in the greatest human fulfilment, and will reap ultimate rewards in heaven.

The act of surrendering is very difficult for those who have a mindset that the battle is lost.

There was a time where I almost lost my faith. The story was shared in Chapter 4 – Realignment and Redirection. When we suffer, we tend to do anything and everything to find a way out of the pain. But sometimes God calls us to walk in our pain for His glory.

- He may be sanctifying us.
- He may be preparing us.
- In the sanctification and preparation, there is strengthening.

The hope of His glory gave me strength to keep moving forward. The freedom of my surrendered pain gave me hope that there would be healing. We can be in the thick of a tangled mess, unable to see much steps ahead, we only see from a limited perspective; however, when we surrender to God's will, in the midst of our pain, we find strength to trust that He is working a beautiful masterpiece in our lives and keeps us going. The next time you cannot see past your suffering, remember that God is with you and He wants to heal you.

He just asks you to surrender your pain to Him and He will give you peace.

CHAPTER 9

SUPPLICATION AND STAND

In your wilderness stage, you cannot afford not to make supplication unto God. Your waiting or trying period demands that you continually offer prayer of supplication to God. It is not the time to be complaining and murmuring. Prayer is very essential. Never stop talking to God about your pain, trials, and challenges.

Ephesians 6: 18 states *"Praying always with all prayer and supplication in the Spirit, and watching thereunto with all perseverance and supplication for all saints"* We come to God in prayer for a variety of reasons—to worship Him, to confess our sins and ask for forgiveness, to thank Him for His blessings, to ask for things for ourselves, and/or to pray for the needs of others. A prayer of supplication is asking God for something. Unlike the prayer of petition, which is praying on behalf of others, the prayer of supplication is generally a request for the person praying.

Time with God is the best place to find strength to press on.

Clearly, prayers of supplication are part of the spiritual battle all Christians are engaged in. Paul exhorts the Philippian church to relieve their anxieties by remaining faithful in prayer, especially prayers of thanksgiving and supplication. This, he concludes, is the formula for ensuring that ***"the peace of God, which passes all understanding, will guard your hearts and your minds in Christ Jesus"*** – Philippians 4: 6 -7

Be careful about nothing; but in everything by prayer and supplication with thanksgiving, let your requests be made known unto God.

In the New Testament, Jesus tells us to ask for our daily bread which falls into the category of prayer of supplication. In addition, Jesus teaches us not to give up praying for what we need. James says that: on the one hand, we do not receive because we do not ask.

On the other hand, we ask and do not receive because we are thinking only of our fleshly desires. Perhaps the best way to approach supplications is to ask God in all honesty as children talking to their kind-hearted Father, but ending with "Your will be done", in full surrender to His will.

Supplication literally means "a request or petition." In spiritual context- a person who makes supplication humbly presents his requests before God with an expectation that He will answer them. Christians are to daily offer their supplications to God in form of thanksgiving and making petition for their needs.

"There should be a parallel between our supplications and our thanksgivings. We ought not to leap in prayer, and limp in praise." ~ Charles Spurgeon

"Prayer is the noble supplication which we lift up to the throne of the Most High. It is the most efficient means to obtain from God the graces which we need." ~ Pier Giorgio Frassati

Be Specific.

I believe God likes that kind of specificity when we talk to Him. When Bartimaeus, the blind beggar, called out to Jesus for help, Jesus said, ***"What do you want me to do for you?"*** *And the blind man said,* ***"My Rabbi . . . I want to see!" Jesus said, "Go, for your faith has healed you"*** (Mark 10:51–52). We do not need to beat about the bush with God. While there may be a time to pray poetically as David did, there are also times to say bluntly, "God, I am so sorry for what I just said," or to say simply, "Jesus, I love You because . . . ."

Being specific with God is a sign of faith because we are acknowledging that we know we are not talking to a far-off Being, but to a real Person who loves us intimately. God is not impressed by a flurry of fanciful words. He is listening to what our heart is saying.

The heart of prayer is prayer from the heart.

Sometimes ago, I read an article which really blessed me. Here is the excerpt:

> *"Life is hard for the villagers who live on a hilly terrain in the Yunnan Province of China. Their main source of food is corn and rice. But in May 2012, a severe drought hit the region and the crops withered. Everyone was worried, and many superstitious practices*

> *were carried out as the people attempted to end the drought. When nothing worked, people started blaming the five Christians in the village for offending the spirits of the ancestors. These five believers gathered to pray. Before long, the sky darkened, and thunder was heard. A heavy downpour started and lasted the whole afternoon and night. The crops were saved! While most of the villagers did not believe God sent the rain, others did and desired to find out more about Him and Jesus".*

In 1 Kings 17 and 18, we also read of a severe drought in Israel. But in this case, we are told, it was a result of God's judgment on His people (17:1). They had begun to worship Baal, the god of the Canaanites, believing that this deity could send the rain for their crops.

Then God, through His prophet, Elijah, showed that He is the one true God who determines when rain falls. Our all-powerful God desires to hear our prayers and answer our pleas. Though we do not always understand His timing or His purposes, God always responds with His best for our lives.

Through prayer, we draw on the power of the infinite God.

Prayer is a critical part of the life of every Christian. Through prayer we encounter and are encountered by God. We are told in Jeremiah "Call to me and I will answer you and tell you great and unsearchable things you do not know." These are powerful words. It is a promise from God. Why then would we not pray? We have many reasons. And even when we do pray, prayer can become just another option for us; something to pick up and put down for our own purposes. But it can and should be so much more.

Prayer is a mighty vehicle for us. It is something we use to carry out the purposes of God. We know prayer can increase our ministry. We know prayer will boost the harvest. We pray so we can know the mind of God. For instance, we pray so we can lead right. We pray so we can work well. We pray so we can preach what it is in the heart of the Father. We pray so we can accomplish what God wants us to accomplish. We pray so we can commune with God.

Prayer and the life of prayer are spiritual practices. I cannot explain them to you. They must be experienced. I saw a myriad of T-shirts and bumper stickers that say, "Prayer changes things." But prayer does not change things. Prayer has no power whatsoever on its own. If simply being enthusiastic about prayer as a powerful vehicle was enough, I could pray to anything and receive an answer. Prayer does not change things; God changes things! I will say it again: It is not prayer or even a life of prayer that brings us power, it is the God to whom we pray who has all power.

Paul said in 1 Thessalonians 5:16–18, *"Rejoice always, pray continually, give thanks in all circumstances; for this is God's will for you in Christ Jesus."* You and I have been called to do something: pray continually. We are to pray without stopping. Prayer is essential in the life of a Christian. Be intentional today that you are going to become a person who prays—a person who maintains a lifestyle of prayer.

Prayer is Conversation with God

Prayer is conversation with one who is always there. Prayer allows us access through Jesus Christ into a conversation with God. God is always seeking a conversation with us. God always greatly desires to communicate with us. So often we use prayer as a vehicle to get us to a desired destination. We need provision, so we pray. We need anointing, so we pray.

We need healing, or deliverance, or cleansing, so we pray. But what if prayer is not the vehicle that brings us *to* our destination, but rather, what if it *is* the destination? Prayer is not simply a step of the journey; prayer is the journey. When we realise this, we begin to understand prayer as a continuous conversation with God, and our relationship with God deepens to new levels.

Fixing Our Thoughts on Jesus

To fix our thoughts and hearts on Jesus, as we are encouraged to do in Hebrews 3:1, is to relate intimately and lovingly to him. It will mean focusing our spiritual eyes and the emotions of our heart on the person of Jesus, not just His position. Fixing our thoughts on Jesus will result in submission to Him. It will mean moving beyond our rational beliefs about the historical Jesus and seeing Him and all that He is, as a contemporary and present Saviour. He can be trusted! So, fix your eyes on Jesus.

Imagine the Saviour sitting on the throne of heaven at the right hand of God. He is the King of kings and the earth is His footstool. Psalm 104:1 tells us that He is robed with honour and majesty. Let the eyes of your heart see the beautiful throne room, His majestic robes and royal stature. Often, you see Christ's position and your thoughts align with the beliefs about the Saviour, but that's not the same as fixing your thoughts on the *person* of Jesus.

Pause now and fix the eyes of your heart on the character and person of Jesus. Imagine Christ saying these words just to you: "I am the One who sits on heaven's throne, but I love to call you my friend (John 15:15). My name is the Most High, the King of all the earth, but you can come to me any time you desire. I am ready to listen to what you have to say. In fact, I lean in, to hear your prayers" (Psalm 47:2; 17:6).

STAND

Ephesians 6: 13 says *"Wherefore take unto you the whole armour of God, that ye may be able to withstand in the evil day, and having done all, to stand."*

I cannot overemphasise that you stand strong in uncertain times, your wilderness and trying period. The enemy will always lure us towards panic and worry if we focus on all that is wrong in this world. Even when we know the truth and believe that God is in control, there can be a lot in this life we might start to feel anxious about. It can still be a daily battle in our hearts, in our minds. When we keep looking all around, we will easily get defeated and lose strength because fear creeps in.

We lose our focus because we are so distracted by all the things that can never really give us strength and hope. God alone can offer us confident peace that can never be found in this life. Choose today, to set your eyes on Him. For if He made all of heaven and earth, surely, He has a sovereign and incredible plan for you and for me. He knows our ways in this journey of life, and He is a "with us" God.

Do not allow yourself to go into a state of depression due to a temporary situation.

What you are going through is because of where you are going to. Therefore stand! ***STAND! STAND!! STAND!!!***

CHAPTER 10

REWARDS OF WAITING ON GOD

Waiting is another important key that makes it possible for God to address the problems we encounter as Christians in life, miraculously. God is a God of miracle. But when you get ahead of Him, you rob Him of an opportunity to prove His power in your life. So, learn to wait.

Waiting on God Is Proof of Trust.

Sometimes in life, challenges, trials, hardships, poverty, ill-health and many other predicaments pose as hindrances or limitations to our individual dream, vision, purpose, goals, family, education, business and happiness, but it is very important to remain calm in the face of all these hurdles of life. Many of us throw in the towel so easily when these moments come crumbling before us, or on us.

The question is "what should one do to remain steadfast, unmovable, unshakable and focused when trusting in the **GOD OF ALL POSSIBLITIES**?" Some may even ask that question 'What is (are) the benefit(s) of trusting and waiting on God for an answer that does not seem to be forthcoming?

God has the power and ability to help you cross over these hurdles of life. Just trust in Him and you will never be ashamed. The storms of life and other many things may come after you but if only you can just hold on and trust God, He will come through for you.

Waiting on God is simply your ability to believe that He holds and directs your life; and without Him, you are nobody. You cannot trust the person you do not know or develop a personal relationship with. When you know someone, it is very easy to build some level of trust with such an individual. This is the main reason why we are supposed to develop an intimacy with God to give us the platform to trust him in the face of life challenges and battles.

Biblically, waiting is not just something we have to do until we get what we want. Waiting is part of the process of becoming who God wants us to be.

Amid all these hurdles, we need to develop our patience and humility to trust in God, trusting in His power and grace to take you through these life challenges. No amount of your challenges can limit God. It may look as if your challenges are limiting you but hey! THEY CANNOT LIMIT YOUR GOD (Numbers 23: 19, Psalm 89.34; Isaiah 14:24)

If only you can wait on God, trust in Him and remain focused in serving Him. He is committed in reshaping your destiny and giving you a TOMORROW that will surely make you forget your YESTERDAY. Romans 8.28.

Your God is more than able to do what He has promised you......All you need to do is to wait on Him, be patient and trust in Him.

Throughout the stories of the Bible, we often find God's people waiting.

- Think of Abraham who had to wait for years, for God to bless him with the son He promised him.
- Think of Noah and the many months he must have worked on the ark, yet he apparently saw no rain when he was constructing the ark. He was possibly ridiculed.
- Think of the anointed David who had to be refined for many 'waiting' years to assume the position of king he was anointed for, since he was a teenager.

- Think of the disciples, taking Jesus at His word by following Him, but having to wait until they were released to do ministry.

What about the followers of God who waited 400 years in silence between the Old Testament and the arrival of Jesus?

Waiting on God is a part of the Christian experience. The waiting times are difficult to endure, especially if you are like me and generally struggle to patiently wait. Show me someone who has grown in their maturity in Christ and I can almost guarantee they have had seasons when they were waiting.

I have learnt, however, some lessons during my own wait. These lessons helped and prepared me when God chose to act in my life.

Are you in a time of waiting? Perhaps, some of these suggestions may help.

Here are 7 things to do while you are waiting on God

1. Prepare your heart

The goal of God in my life is to transform me into the image of His Son. He wants my heart and character more than great activities I could do for Him. The silent times are some of the best times to seek the heart of God. During the waiting period, I found that I needed to increase my prayer and study time, preparing my heart to receive God's instructions.

2. Learn all you can

I learn more from the struggles of life than I do from the easy times of life. The same can be true through the times of waiting for God to move. God reveals His character to us as we wait. I found myself reading more of the Psalms during times of waiting. They remind me of God's presence even during days of silence.

3. Watch for His activity

Just because it seems that God is silent does not mean He is being still, doing nothing.

God is always doing something, even when I cannot tell what it is. I have learnt to be watchful for the hidden activity of God.

4. Stay active with what you know to be doing

The Bible is clear on some things I should always do. – love my neighbour, look out for "the least of these", "make disciples" – just to name a few. Waiting times do not mean doing nothing. It may be in the "doing something" that we discover God has been waiting to bless us.

5. Listen for His voice or the voice of others He sends

Isaiah 30:20-21 talks about a "*voice*" saying "*this is the way – walk in it*" during the "*days of adversity*." This is an important reminder. I have learnt to listen for His voice, understanding that the more I know Him personally, the more I will hear even His softest whisper. Many times, God is trying to speak to us whether through His written Word (which seems to be the dominant way He speaks), or through other people in our lives, or through the circumstances of our lives. Often there are consistent themes I keep "hearing", but it takes me a while to actually process them.

6. Heal from past hurts – if needed

Many times, the silent periods in my walk with God come after very difficult periods. At times, I have learnt that I could not hear God because my emotions are clouded with the pain of my past. In those days, what I needed most was to heal my emotions so I could think clearly, discern His voice, and prepare for His next assignment for me. This may take processing hurts with others, extending forgiveness, or admitting sin to renew my closeness with God.

7. Pray without ceasing

Prayer is my personal connection to God. As long as I am praying, I am less likely to worry and more likely to walk by faith. Praying without ceasing does not mean I do nothing except pray, but it means I carry a faithful attitude – a heart of prayer – into everything I do. I remain keenly aware of His presence through the Spirit of God, so that when He speaks, I have the best possible opportunity to hear Him.

Here Are 17 Rewards for Waiting on God

1. Waiting reveals patience. Patience is a seed that always produces a desired harvest. Patience is always rewarded. (Luke 21:19; Hebrews 11:11.).

2. Waiting time is not wasted time. *"But let patience have her perfect work, that ye may be perfect and entire, wanting nothing,"* (James 1:4).

3. Waiting guarantees favourable results. *"The Lord is good unto them that wait for Him, to the soul that seeketh Him. It is good that a man should both hope and quietly wait for the salvation of the Lord,"* (Lamentations 3:25-26).

4. Waiting is learning time. As long as you are learning, you are not losing. The integrity of the General demands that he qualifies his soldiers for the battle. God will prune, train, and teach you in your waiting time. (Psalm 144:1.) Your flesh will react to waiting. It hates waiting. It wants action. It pursues activity. Waiting forces your flesh to die.

5. Waiting will reveal the true motives and intentions of those around you. Motives are not always easily discerned. Therefore, Joseph was willing to wait before revealing his identity to his brothers when they approached him for food during a famine in the land. Joseph's brothers did not know he was related to them. He knew them. Undoubtedly, the desire to reveal himself was intense. But he knew the limitations of intuition. He remembered the excitement of sharing his dream with his brothers only to be sold into slavery because of it.

6. Waiting reveals that you trust God but willing to test men. It is Biblical: *"Some trust in chariots,*

and some in horses: but we will remember the name of the Lord our God," (Psalm20:7). You see, the wrong people can keep their mistakes covered for long periods of time but waiting forces the truth to emerge.

7. Waiting enables you to gather accurate and untainted information. The quality of your information determines the quality of your decisions. And the quality of your decisions determines the quality of your life.

8. Waiting brings you truth.

9. More waiting brings you more truth.

10. Enough waiting brings you enough truth.

11. You will never see the hand Of God if you keep trusting the hand of man in your life. Unwillingness to wait for supernatural provision will produce tragedies every time.

12. Waiting is a weapon Satan dreads for you to ever discover. "*Lest Satan should get an advantage of us: for we are not ignorant of his devices*," (2 Corinthians 2:11).

13. Waiting on God's timing will produce the desired results of your assignment. Time is the hidden and mysterious seed in an uncommon harvest. "*The Lord is good unto them that wait for Him, to the soul that seeketh Him*," (Lamentations 3:25).

14. Waiting Reveals the weaknesses of impatient enemies.

15. Waiting provides God the time to interrupt any attack on your life with a miraculous deliverance.

16. Waiting increases strength. "*He giveth power to the faint; and to them that have no might He increaseth strength. Even the youths shall faint and be weary, and the young men shall utterly fall: But they that wait upon the Lord shall renew*

their strength; they shall mount up with wings as eagles they shall run, and not be weary ;and they shall walk, and not faint,"(Isaiah 40:29-31).

17. Waiting gives time for others to become what wisdom is producing within them. Patience is the willingness to assign time to work on a solution, in your life and in the life of others important to you.

- Patience produces exceptional friendships.
- Patience produces great marriages.
- Patience will produce what money cannot provide.
- Patience has turned around weak and unhealthy people through exercise and focus; producing powerful, strong bodies.

Remember, your greatest blessings, for now, may come after your longest waiting...mine have!

CHAPTER 11

NEVER EVER DO IT

Life could be difficult at times, especially when we are going through wilderness experience or period of process. During those times, there would be feelings of quitting and hoping the pain would disappear because we believe we could no longer endure the ordeal.

You must have heard the saying, "***Quitters never win, winners never quit***". If you quit the pain or the process God is taking you through, you will never experience the result of the process or the pain. There is always a purpose in the mind of God for taking you through the process or the wilderness experience, and if you quit, you may never experience the reality of the promise.

If you quit on the process, you are quitting on the result.

Emotional feeling of giving up or quitting is common to everyone. There will always be temptation at one time or the other to throw in the towel. I remember during my waiting on God for my breakthrough, there were times when I really felt like giving up.

I believed there was no way I could endure the process again. About six times, I thought of relocating to Nigeria if the UK immigration department would not grant me a legal stay in the UK. Each time I went to God in prayer, He kept reminding me that His grace is sufficient for me.

At times I had to encourage myself in the Lord as David did, worshipped and sang praises to Him. I also prayed for renewed strength.

QUITTING DEFINED:

- To stop seeing somebody
- To stop doing something
- To stop going to a place
- To free yourself, withdraw
- To depart from, leave something, abandon, relinquish, discontinue
- To walk away from something

It is a feeling that all believers have, no matter how spiritual we are. God's Word admonished us against giving up. We have scriptures to learn from.

For example, 1 Cor 10 :13 says *"There hath no temptation taken you but such as is common to man: but God is faithful, who will not suffer you to be tempted above that ye are able; but will with the temptation also make a way to escape, that ye may be able to bear it."*

You need to understand that for every trial you are going through, God is very much aware of it and He knows you can bear it. God is faithful to those He has called. God is faithful in times of trials. God is faithful in fulfilling His promises. God is faithful in times of suffering. God is faithful even when we are unfaithful. Hence you must never ever try to give up or quit. God is ever faithful.

REASONS WHY PEOPLE GIVE UP OR QUIT.

1. Unfulfilled legitimate desire. We all have desires in life and if it seems there is a delay with the fulfilment, and our heart desires are not granted on time, we tend to give up.

Proverbs 13: 12 says *"Hope deferred maketh the heart sick: but when the desire cometh, it is a tree of life."*

Psalm 145: 19 *"He will fulfil the desire of them that fear him: he also will hear their cry and will save them."*

Psalm 37:4 *"Delight thyself also in the LORD; and he shall give thee the desires of thine heart."*

2. When circumstances remain unchanged or get worse, feelings of throwing in the towel come to mind, several times.

3. Lies of the Enemy- Satan making people to give up and saying to them that is the best thing to do. One of Satan's methods or scheme is to make you feel that you will never come out of a mess or it will get worse. Satan the tempter, tempts believers. He works in a cunning way to weaken the hearts of people. He is very good at getting people upset about themselves, and eventually giving up during trials.

2 Cor 2: 11 says *"Lest Satan should get an advantage of us: for we are not ignorant of his devices.". You need to resist the devil, persist and persevere.*

Ephesians 4: 27 *"Neither give place to the devil.".*

4. Seeing things from man's angle instead of God's perspective. Hence the need to pray for

God to open your eyes. Psalm 13: 3 says *"Consider and hear me, O LORD my God: lighten mine eyes, lest I sleep the sleep of death"*. Do not listen to the lies of the Enemy. God has the final say. – Numbers 23 : 19 says *" God is not a man, that he should lie; neither the son of man, that he should repent: hath he said, and shall he not do it? or hath he spoken, and shall he not make it good?"*

Romans 3: 4 *"God forbid: yea, let God be true, but every man a liar; as it is written, That thou mightest be justified in thy sayings, and mightest overcome when thou art judged."*

1 Sam 16 : 17 *"But the LORD said unto Samuel, Look not on his countenance, or on the height of his stature; because I have refused him: for the LORD seeth not as man seeth; for man looketh on the outward appearance, but the LORD looketh on the heart"*

Jeremiah 32: 17 *"Ah Lord GOD! behold, thou hast made the heaven and the earth by thy great power and stretched out arm, and there is nothing too hard for thee:..."*

Jeremiah 32: 27 *"Behold, I am the LORD, the God of all flesh: is there anything too hard for me?"*

Luke 18: 27 "*And he said, the things which are impossible with men are possible with God."*

Joseph saw from God's eye according to Genesis 50: 20 – *"But as for you, ye thought evil against me; but God meant it unto good, to bring to pass, as it is this day, to save much people alive."* Develop a sharp spiritual eyesight by seeing the way God sees.

5. Many pressures and problems that are exerted upon us. There is grace to carry these many problems and pressures when are under too many pressures.

6. Negative influence from seemingly loved ones, also wrong words of advice that may lead

to giving up. Exodus 23: 2 *"Thou shalt not follow a multitude to do evil; neither shalt thou speak in a cause to decline after many to wrest judgment"*

7. Disappointment from previous result obtained. When disappointments come knocking on the door, feelings of giving up.

8. Comparing oneself with others. Never compare yourself with other people.

9. Feelings of "time is gone, …one cannot make it again." FAIL simply means First Attempt In Learning.

10. Subscribing to traditional ideas, culture at times, oversubscribing to it. Subscription to it makes you feel like giving up.

Giving up is a choice. So also, is standing firm, unshakable in the midst of trying period. The choice you make to quit is also the choice you can make not to quit. The choice to quit is yours, the choice not to quit is also yours.

Let us consider few reasons to hold on and not give up-

REASONS NOT TO GIVE UP

1. The choice not to quit is at your disposal and the supernatural manifestation of God shows up for you like never when you do not. The moment you choose to be unshakable, His power comes, supernatural power and grace of God comes for you. The choice helps the grace to be poured.

2. God is not happy with to those who quit, turn back, or give up. God sees you as misfit if you quit. Luke 9:62 *"And Jesus said unto him, no man, having put his hand to the plough, and looking back, is fit for the kingdom of God". Hebrews 10:38 – 39 "Now the just shall live by faith: but if any man draw back, my soul shall have no pleasure in him. But we are not of them who draw back unto perdition; but of them that believe to the saving of the soul."*

3. Jesus was a perfect example. He never gave up when He was tempted to give up. To be tempted is not a sin, to give in to temptation is a sin.

Hebrews 12:2 *"Looking unto Jesus the author and finisher of our faith; who for the joy that was set before him endured the cross, despising the shame, and is set down at the right hand of the throne of God". Isaiah 41:10 "Fear thou not; for I am with thee: be not dismayed; for I am thy God: I will strengthen thee; yea, I will help thee; yea, I will uphold thee with the right hand of my righteousness."*

4. Consider those who give up and compare who did not in the Bible. Both had a choice. If you want God's power to intervene, make a choice not to quit.

5. For what will you quit for? What next? What you will do next, will it be better than what you want to quit from? To whom and what will you quit to?

6. Do not quit because what you are going through is a stage, season, phase of life that will soon pass over; it is a period, a stage that will soon pass. Romans 8: 18 "***For I reckon that the sufferings of this present time are not worthy to be compared with the glory which shall be revealed in us.***"

7. You have not reached the place of promise- the height you need to get to. Hold on! Do not give up! God's eye is guiding you and will guide you through your lonely path. Ps. 32:8 "***I will instruct thee and teach thee in the way which thou shalt go: I will guide thee with mine eye.***"

CHAPTER 12

PERFORMANCE

Without the process, the performance will not carry the weight of the promise. The performance is the manifestation of whatever God has promised you, but it does not happen overnight, hence the process you are in is of a necessity. Therefore, you need to embrace the process to see the performance of the promise.

The Scriptural verse - Romans 4 :21 *"And being fully persuaded that, what he had promised, he was able also to perform."* serves as a reminder that God will bring to performance whatever He has promised. You have a responsibility to believe beyond any doubt that He will surely perform that promise. You will need to be fully persuaded, having a deep conviction that He will surely perform that promise. The performance will not be manifested or come to pass if you shy away from the process, He would take you through and you cannot afford to bypass the process stage which precedes the performance stage, if you do, you cannot experience the reality of the performance.

There is always a test before promotion as far as God is concerned. God will test you before He can trust you. Reading through the Bible, God had to work in His people, refining their character and humbling them with challenges they faced before He could entrust them with what He covenanted for them. They were all put to test through the trials and tribulations they faced.

Abraham, Joseph, Isaac, Paul, even our Lord and Saviour- Jesus Christ, were all tested before God trusted them.

In our world today, if you looked and studied closely the people God is working His manifestations through, you would agree with me that all of them went through process and after this came the promotion or performance. You need to understand that your process stage is personal and unique to you.

And being fully persuaded that, what He had promised He was able also to perform- Romans 4:21

It might not be visible to others however it is visible to God, your Father. It is not everybody who will be aware of your trying times except few people that are close to you. Guess what, the performance and the manifestation of His promise is always visible. Everyone can see it.

Just like a building, the foundation is not visible to everyone, but only the main building is visible, attractive and beautiful. Without the foundation there cannot be a building.

The foundation is what is holding the building. So, your process can be compared to the foundation while the promise is the building plan and the performance is the real building, which is what everyone can see and give glory to God for.

The angel told Mary in Luke 1: 45, *"blessed is she that believed for there shall be a performance of those things which were told her from the Lord."* You see, you just need to believe that whatever God has promised you in His Word or through a confirmed prophecy, that there shall surely be a performance of those promises.

Thus, it is very important that you have a Word from God which you can lay hold on, and understand what His Will is, for your life. You cannot afford to put your faith in what is contrary to God's will for your life. You cannot afford to believe God for whatever that is not His Will for your life.

Why is it that process must always precede performance? Have you ever thought of this? Process must always precede performance because it is a prerequisite. The process we go through is what build in us the Godly character, virtues and spiritual stamina needed to sustain the performance.

In other words, God will first prepare you for what He has already prepared for you. God allows a 'new you' to be developed first so that you can sustain the performance of the promise and scripture. He wants to refine our character before He releases the blessings.

There is no one God uses without first taking them through process. Moses wanted to deliver his people- Israelites, with his own might and wisdom, God had to prepare him for forty years before he was used powerfully by God to deliver Israel from the hand of the enemies. God is ever faithful to do or perform that which He has promised you or said to you through His Word.

Hebrews 10: 23 says *"Let us hold fast the profession of our faith without wavering; for He is faithful that promised."*

The promise of God's unfailing presence with us is the key to living with confidence and contentment. God's promises and His faithfulness will last through all time and eternity.

What will God perform or what will He bring to performance?

1. **His promises** – 1 Cor 1: 20 *"For all the promises of God in him are yea, and in him Amen, unto the glory of God by us."*

Joshua 21: 45 *"Not one of all the Lord's good promises to Israel failed; everyone was fulfilled."* (NIV)

Joshua 23: 14 *"Now I am about to go the way of all the earth. You know with all your heart and soul that not one of all the good promises the*

Lord your God gave you has failed. Every promise has been fulfilled; not one has failed" (NIV)

2. **His purpose -** Proverbs 19: 21 *"Many are the plans in a person's heart, but it is the Lord's purpose that prevails."*

Psalm 57: 2 *"I cry out to God Most High, to God who will fulfil his purpose for me."* (NLT)

Rev 11: 15 *"The seventh angel sounded his trumpet, and there were loud voices in heaven, which said: "The kingdom of the world has become the kingdom of our Lord and of his Messiah, and he will reign for ever and ever."*

3. **His plans -** Jeremiah 29: 11 *"For I know the plans I have for you," declares the Lord, "plans to prosper you and not to harm you, plans to give you hope and a future."*

4. **Your prayers -** 1 Peter 3 : 12 " *For the eyes of the Lord are over the righteous, and his ears are*

open unto their prayers: but the face of the Lord is against them that do evil."

John 14: 13 *"And whatsoever ye shall ask in my name, that will I do, that the Father may be glorified in the Son."*

Matthew 21: 22 *"And all things, whatsoever ye shall ask in prayer, believing, ye shall receive"*

5. **Your desires and expectations -** Proverbs 23: 18 *"For surely there is an end; and thine expectation shall not be cut off."*

Psalm 37: 4 *"Delight thyself also in the LORD; and he shall give thee the desires of thine heart."*

Proverbs 13: 12 "*Hope deferred maketh the heart sick: but when the desire cometh, it is a tree of life."*

6. **Your thoughts -** Ephesians 3: 20 *"Now unto him that is able to do exceedingly abundantly*

above all that we ask or think, according to the power that worketh in us"

Proverbs 23: 7 *"For as he thinketh in his heart, so is he: Eat and drink, saith he to thee; but his heart is not with thee"*

Philippians 4 : 8 *"Finally, brethren, whatsoever things are true, whatsoever things are honest, whatsoever things are just, whatsoever things are pure, whatsoever things are lovely, whatsoever things are of good report; if there be any virtue, and if there be any praise, think on these things."*

7. **Your declaration and confessions** – Proverbs 18: 20 -21 *"A man's belly shall be satisfied with the fruit of his mouth; and with the increase of his lips shall he be filled. Death and life are in the power of the tongue: and they that love it shall eat the fruit thereof."*

Job 22: 28 *"Thou shalt also decree a thing, and it shall be established unto thee: and the light shall shine upon thy ways."*

Romans 10: 8 – 10 *"But what saith it? The word is nigh thee, even in thy mouth, and in thy heart: that is, the word of faith, which we preach; That if thou shalt confess with thy mouth the Lord Jesus, and shalt believe in thine heart that God hath raised him from the dead, thou shalt be saved. For with the heart man believeth unto righteousness; and with the mouth confession is made unto salvation."*

8. **Your faith -** Mark 11 : 23 -24 *" For verily I say unto you, That whosoever shall say unto this mountain, Be thou removed, and be thou cast into the sea; and shall not doubt in his heart, but shall believe that those things which he saith shall come to pass; he shall have whatsoever he saith. Therefore, I say unto you, what things so ever ye desire, when ye pray, believe that ye receive them, and ye shall have them."*

Matthew 17 : 20 *" And Jesus said unto them, Because of your unbelief: for verily I say unto you, If ye have faith as a grain of mustard seed, ye shall say unto this mountain, Remove hence to yonder place; and it shall remove; and nothing shall be impossible unto you"*

2 Cor 5: 7 "… *For we walk by faith, not by sight:…"*

9. **Your salvation** – 1 Peter 1: 9 *"Receiving the end of your faith, even the salvation of your souls."*

Psalm 62: 2 "*Truly he is my rock and my salvation; he is my fortress, I will never be shaken."*

10. **The works of your hand** – Psalm 90: 17 "*And let the beauty of the LORD our God be upon us: and establish thou the work of our hands upon us; yea, the work of our hands establish thou it."*

Deuteronomy 28 : 12 "*The LORD shall open unto thee his good treasure, the heaven to give the rain unto thy land in his season, and to bless all the work of thine hand: and thou shalt lend unto many nations, and thou shalt not borrow.*"

Psalm 1: 3 "*And he shall be like a tree planted by the rivers of water, that bringeth forth his fruit in his season; his leaf also shall not wither; and whatsoever he doeth shall prosper.*"

FINAL THOUGHTS

John 12: 24 says "*Verily, verily, I say unto you, except a corn of wheat fall into the ground and die, it abideth alone: but if it die, it bringeth forth much fruit*"

In the journey of destiny, there will be a need to die. What do you need to die to? You need to die to self, vainglory, affairs of this world- those things that do not bring glory to God.

Why do you need to die? You will need to die because of what God has destined to come to manifestation in your life. To live, something must die. The only way this can happen is through process. Therefore, God will take you through a process in the journey of destiny.

Process is the period God empties you of yourself, so that He alone can be able to fill you. A time that He will strip you of all your personal agenda, selfishness and from those things that are taking His place in your life. So therefore, it is more about you, and God changing your focus to Him and to trust Him totally. Why? Because 'process' is a way we trust God even if He does not come through.

God had to take Joseph through process by changing His focus from himself to God. When Joseph had a dream, he was eager to brag about the dream to his brothers. His narration of the dream was "I" centred, not "God" centred, thus he had to be taken through process for his focus to change to God, totally dependent on God.

When it seemed like freedom was around the corner through the chief butler whose dream he interpreted, the Bible mentions that the chief butler forgot about Joseph after he left the prison. The reason was simply because the process had not finished, and he had not totally learnt his lesson.

It was after his focus had changed to God that the process came to an end. Afterwards, promotion and performance followed. His process was not complete until his conversation and response was geared towards giving God all the glory. In Genesis 41: 16 which says "*And Joseph answered Pharaoh, saying, it is not in me: God shall give Pharaoh an answer of peace.* This was the turning point in Joseph's life and where his process came to an end. His focus before this time was I, I, I, as if he had the ability without God.

At this point, he had an insight that it is not about him. His answer then changed to God, in other words, he recognised that it can only be by God, hence his answer was different from all his previous responses. As soon as this took place, his process came to an end and the performance

of the promise was manifested. Verse 39 – 43 - *And Pharaoh said unto Joseph, Forasmuch as God hath shewed thee all this, there is none so discreet and wise as thou art:*
Thou shalt be over my house, and according unto thy word shall all my people be ruled: only in the throne will I be greater than thou. And Pharaoh said unto Joseph, See, I have set thee over all the land of Egypt. And Pharaoh took off his ring from his hand, and put it upon Joseph's hand, and arrayed him in vestures of fine linen, and put a gold chain about his neck; And he made him to ride in the second chariot which he had; and they cried before him, Bow the knee: and he made him ruler over all the land of Egypt.

You need to understand that the whole essence of the process is to make God our total reliance and dependency. He must remain our focus. It is then essential that process must always precedes performance of the promise. In dry times, we learn to seek God for who He is rather than what He can do for us.

Hebrews 12:2 says *"Looking unto Jesus the author and finisher of our faith; who for the joy that was set before him endured the cross, despising the shame, and is set down at the right hand of the throne of God"*. The scripture here states clearly that enduring pain is one of the ways, perhaps the main way God works His grace deeply into our lives. The transformation of your soul comes through process. That is why God must take us through our own unique process.

There is a glory God wants to reveal in and through you, and that can only come to pass through process with pain, sufferings, disappointments, betrayals, trials etc. As Romans 8: 18 puts it: *For I reckon that the sufferings of this present time are not worthy to be compared with the glory which shall be revealed in us.*

Your process is for a phase and there is need to endure it and remain focused on God. Your perspective and response to it matters to its outcome. Therefore, you must guard your heart and feed your inner man with the Word.

2 Cor 4: 16 – 18 says "*For which cause we faint not; but though our outward man perish, yet the inward man is renewed day by day. For our light affliction, which is but for a moment, worketh for us a far more exceeding and eternal weight of glory; While we look not at the things which are seen, but at the things which are not seen: for the things which are seen are temporal; but the things which are not seen are eternal.*"

Whatever you might be going through now, see it as God preparing you for what He had already prepared for you. The wilderness is not punishment. It is God's preparation for His promise to be performed in your life. He had to process me for Him to build in me the necessary virtue, character, and spiritual stamina I needed to sustain the performance of His promise concerning my life.

For the 10 years that I did not earn any income in the UK, of course the UK government did support me and my family for those years, God indeed taught me how to totally rely, depend and trust in Him. He taught me why patience and faith are necessary in my walk with Him. Let me conclude by saying that to walk with God, to experience the performance of His promise, you need to have patience and faith. Patience in terms of the ability to wait for God's appointed time, not your own expected time. Faith is believing that He is ever faithful to do that which He has promised.

You need to embrace the season and the process He is taking you through. Your focus must change from that which you are trusting and believing Him to do in your life to Him alone. There are somethings you can only learn in a storm, that is why your waiting time is a learning period.

Anyone that has not had serious challenges and trials can be boastful in himself and such is living an untested life. Courageous men and women are made by the challenges they faced and overcome.

Whatever you are going through is not new, it is to make, refine, purge, and transform you. Do your best to win and do not ever, ever, ever, I mention it again and again - do not ever give up.

How to Survive your Process

1. Have a right attitude during a time of crisis. Count it all joy remembering that murmuring and complaining is the sound of weakness that draws the attention of the enemy to its prey. Rejoice because you have the victory and God is going to take the initiatives of the enemy and producc something unprecedented from it.
2. Make sure you are in contact with information from right people who have gone ahead of you. Tenacity is important but not enough. The right information is crucial, knowing what to do.

3. Purpose in your heart to Totally Obey and Honor God
4. Do Not Rob God of His Due Praise/ Worship, because of your pain. Rather, use it as a catalyst to a Closer Intimacy with God.
5. Do Not Trust your Feelings/Emotions. They will Fluctuate.
6. Admit and Own up to your Mistakes, but Do Not let them Redefine Who you are. God has Not changed His Mind concerning You
7. Expect to be ostracized, talked about, and Marginalized by many, but Do Not Lose Sight of what God tell you. He is working out His Purpose in you.
8. Always have a "This too shall pass" and a "Romans 8:28" Attitude.
9. Remember He Loves You Unconditionally and Can Not Lie. Your Best is still yet to come.
10. Finally, cast your care upon the Lord. The very thing Satan is threatening you with, place it in the hands of the Lord

and continually declare His promises to eliminate every thought of anxiety and imagination of a wrong outcome. Things are never as bad as the enemy is escalating it to be in your mind.

You are a Survivor, You Aint Seen Nothing Yet.

100 LIFE TRANSFORMATION QUOTES TO MEDITATE UPON

1. In the same way gold and silver are refined by fire, the Lord purifies your heart by the test and trials of life.
2. Process is what builds in you the necessary character, virtue, and spiritual stamina to sustain the performance of the promise.
3. The whole essence of the process is to make God your reliance, dependence and focus.
4. Transforming yourself comes through process.
5. Process is a way you trust God even if He does not do anything for you.

6. Process is a way your trust in God is built and it allows you to trust God.
7. We are interested in the destination; God is interested in both the journey and destination.
8. Process is more about you, and God changing your focus to Him.
9. Process is the period God empties you of yourself so that God can fill you of Him.
10. God is interested in building your character than making you happy or comfortable.
11. The wilderness or process is your journey to a promise fulfilled. If you have received a promise from God, be rest assured, you will be tested in the wilderness.
12. Going through the wilderness does not mean you are off course. God wants to use the wilderness season to develop you into someone who can walk in everything He has planned for your life.

13. The lack of a thing is not denial on the side of God. God is more concerned with 'making' you before 'giving' you things.
14. God is more committed to your long-term transformation than short-term comfort.
15. Do not allow yourself to go into a state of depression due to a temporary situation.
16. Courage is not having the strength to go on. It is going on when you do not have the strength.
17. Stay with the program He is preparing you for what He has prepared for you.
18. Patience is the force you need so as to walk with God successfully when challenges or difficulties come in your life.
19. We are not entitled to pain-free, trouble-free life. Embracing this will ease the collision between expectation and reality.
20. Not all storms come to disrupt your life, some come to clear your path.
21. God is taking you somewhere. But it takes seeing and knowing where, to be

able to endure where you are and what you are going through right now.

22. What situation are you looking at in your life that is so bad, and you think God cannot rescue you from it? You must decide whether you trust your situation more than you trust God. He is your constant Help in time of trouble. Trust Him!
23. People admire the gain, but they do not want the pain.
24. You are not alone. You are just in a place of separation because God is preparing you for greatness.
25. Stay patient and trust your journey.
26. Challenges are what make life interesting and overcoming them make life meaningful. You are strong enough to overcome your challenges.
27. Failure is the opportunity to begin again more intelligently. Do not be afraid to fail.

28. When the waiting period is over, patience and endurance is developed. Then you will see the promises of God unfold. God's timing is perfect. Bigger and better things are on the way.
29. You do not grow and learn anything when everything is easy.
30. When the blessing is delayed, God is working on you and your character. The blessing is the reward that comes after you have learnt obedience through the things you suffered while waiting.
31. Even Jesus had to learn obedience through the things He suffered, although He is the Son of God. Whatever you might be going through now, ask the Lord to help you learn to be obedient to Him in that suffering. The blessing is the reward for your obedience.
32. To live, something must die. To give birth, a mother has to endure the suffering of the birth process.
33. Before God promotes us, He takes us through pain to purify our hearts, deepen

our dependence on Him and impart spiritual wisdom.

34. Before the resurrection, was the pain of the cross.
35. Pain comes before promotion.
36. You may be going through fire, but God will bring you out on the other side, better than you were before.
37. Painfully, suffering is almost a prerequisite if we are going to be of much use to other people. It makes us far more compassionate.
38. Character is not built in pleasure. Character is built in pains.
39. Do not downgrade your dream to match your reality. Upgrade your faith to match your destiny.
40. Nothing that has happened to you is a surprise to God. You have got to take the hand you have been dealt with and make the most of it.

41. No matter how stormy it becomes amid the earth, those who consistently act on the Word would continue to stand.

42. You are stronger than what is confronting you. You are more than equal to the battle. What will collapse you will never confront you. God did not bring you this far to leave you halfway into your destiny. You will finish well.

43. Where you are coming from should not disturb what God wants to do with you NOW.

44. Where you are now is not as important as where you are going.

45. What you say in time of trouble is determined by a prepared heart from meditation of the WORD.

46. God opens doors to preparedness, not just to prayers.

47. Never use the situation happening to you to rate whether God loves you or accepts you. GOD LOVES YOU.

48. You never realise how much you have grown until adversity returns for an encore.

49. Oftentimes, we pray for open doors but never pray for, and focus on the discipline and preparation of excellence that will keep us in the room once we walk through the door. We want the reward but not the process.

50. No matter your level of faith, if you do not add patience to faith, your expectation may be cut off.

51. Your depths of faith in God speaks loudest during trials and tribulations.

52. The waiting period between when God answers your prayers and when you receive is where Christian character development occurs.

53. There is nothing you need that God cannot do. However, you need to share in His desires. His goal is to get you to a place where you and He will be on the same page.

54. Waiting for a miracle or a breakthrough should not stop you from being productive with time.

55. The grace of God is a radical agent that transforms us from inside out.

56. It takes the inner strength of the Holy Spirit to rejoice in adversity. Rejoice! Rejoice! Rejoice!

57. The devil is trying to use what you are going through to knock you out of your divine assignments.

58. It does not matter if the storm started by the hand of the enemy, it has to pass through the hand of God.

59. God will build your character so you can thrive in your calling. Do not run from the trials. They are not detours – they are training ground.

60. Today's pain is tomorrow's triumph. Your setback today can be turned to your comeback. Never give up!

61. God's plan will always be more beautiful than your disappointments. Be patient and thank God.

62. Not all storms come to simply disrupt your life. In the very midst of adversity, God is removing the dysfunctions and bringing about restoration and order.

63. Believe it or not, God's number one priority is not to make you happy, fulfilled or to have everything go your way. His primary agenda for your life is to make you be like His Son.

64. There is a way you will handle a case or situation if you have passed through it before.

65. Your process period is not a wasted time but a time to gather wisdom to help others during their own trying time.

66. Trust the process God is taking you through. You cannot experience the performance of the promise without the process.

67. Allow God to process you for that promise to come to performance. Therefore, trust the process.
68. Let God prepare you for it. You are not qualified for what you are not prepared for.
69. You cannot have the promise without the process.
70. Welcome your challenges as character-building experiences, learn from them and rise above them.
71. The wilderness is not meant to be a time to defeat, but of victory.
72. Sometimes your current reality may not sync with your revealed destiny. Hold on to the evidence of things not seen.
73. The fight has nothing to do with WHERE you are, but WHERE you are going.
74. Be thankful for the struggles you go through. They make you stronger and wiser. Do not let them break you, let them make you.

75. The beauty of your faith in God is seen when you wait for Him to do what he says He will do.
76. Wait patiently for God and allow Him to prepare you while waiting.
77. You must endure where you are now because of where God is taking you.
78. You do not develop courage by being happy every day. You develop it by surviving difficult times and challenging adversity.
79. It is not the mountain you conquer but yourself.
80. Stay in your process, but never miss the wisdom therein, it is the security of your future.
81. The process is greater than the destination, the wisdom of the process delivers you from the foolishness that comes with arrival.
82. Process is very painful but necessary for your growth and our relationship with God. Allow God to process you.

83. Whatever you are passing through in God is because there is a place you are going to. Stand strong. You will get there.
84. What you planned might not have worked, but hang in there in faith, what He planned would soon appear. Those that wait for Him never see shame.
85. Life with God is not immunity from difficulties, but peace in difficulties.
86. God will not bless you with anything you do not have the capacity to manage. That is why He will allow you to go through processes first.
87. Through Christ, we can be as content in dry times as we are in abundance.
88. You are waiting for God to show up, but He is waiting for you to grow up. As you grow in His knowledge, He shows up.
89. God uses the wilderness to shape you, so the promise land will not break you.
90. Pick a scripture that addresses your situation and take a stand on it and never waver forever.

91. Your time with God is the foundation for everything else in your life. Seek His face, not His hands.

92. Your confession during confusion is the conclusion of your condition.

93. It is you, not God, who determines your level of intimacy with Him. In other words, you are as close to God as you want to be.

94. You grow when you truly believe that God is good, does good and works all things together for your good and for His glory.

95. When God is hiding you, you may feel like a failure.

96. Crushing is not the end. You must begin to appreciate the seemingly unfruitful stages of your inception. For it is in those moments where harvest is cultivated.

97. Pain is not prophecy of your destruction. Although, pain orientates, you are not decimated, instead you are made

stronger. Remember God's promises and let your heart take courage.

98. Just because you took longer than others, does not mean you failed. Remember that!

99. Do not run from the process that leads to your promotion.

100. It is impossible to get to the end if you quit in the middle. Your greatest days are not behind you; they are ahead of you. If you are still breathing, there is no reason to stop. Keep pressing on!

www.ingramcontent.com/pod-product-compliance
Lightning Source LLC
LaVergne TN
LVHW091049080826
845145LV00002B/682

* 9 7 8 0 9 5 5 0 6 7 9 4 5 *